SEATTLE'S STREETCAR ERA

Route 21 Phinney car #535 southbound at Westlake and Pine, 1940. Streetcars served the heart of Seattle's retail business district but also had to contend with heavy auto traffic, as this 1940 scene shows. The two-story flatiron building is gone, but the Frederick and Nelson building (now Nordstrom) behind it survives, as does the Medical Dental Building on the left. *PNRA image WWASMR-21-053.*

This illustrated history has been made possible through the generous support of the Pacific Northwest Railroad Archive, which provided scans of the historic streetcar photographs and extensive research materials on individual streetcar routes and the streetcar fleet.

SEATTLE'S STREETCAR ERA

AN ILLUSTRATED HISTORY
1884–1941

MIKE BERGMAN

Washington State University Press
Pullman, Washington

Washington State University Press
PO Box 645910
Pullman, WA 99164-5910
Phone: 800-354-7360
Email: wsupress@wsu.edu
Website: wsupress.wsu.edu

First printing 2021

Library of Congress Cataloging-in-Publication Data

Names: Bergman, Mike, 1950- author.
Title: Seattle's streetcar era : an illustrated history, 1884-1941 / Mike Bergman.
Description: Pullman, Washington : Washington State University Press, [2021] | Includes bibliographical references and index.
Identifiers: LCCN 2021033637 | ISBN 9780874224078 (hardcover)
Subjects: LCSH: Cable cars (Streetcars)--Washington (State)--Seattle--History. | Street-railroads--Washington (State)--Seattle--History. | Trolley buses--Washington (State)--Seattle--History. | Electric railroads--Cars--Washington (State)--Seattle--History. | Urban transportation--Washington (State)--Seattle--History.
Classification: LCC TF725.S4 B47 2021 | DDC 385.509797--dc23
LC record available at https://lccn.loc.gov/2021033637

The Washington State University Pullman campus is located on the homelands of the Niimíipuu (Nez Perce) Tribe and the Palus people. We acknowledge their presence here since time immemorial and recognize their continuing connection to the land, to the water, and to their ancestors. WSU Press is committed to publishing works that foster a deeper understanding of the Pacific Northwest and the contributions of its Native peoples.

On the cover: Route 30 car #573 at Sunset Hill terminal, NW Sixty-fourth Street and Thirty-sixth Avenue NW, 1939. Originally called the Ballard Beach line, Route 30 ended at this turnaround wye with a sweeping view of Puget Sound and the Olympic Mountains. James A. Turner, photographer. Cover design by Brad Norr Design.

Contents

Illustrations

Maps

Foreword

Bob Wodnik

Mike Bergman's book, *Seattle's Streetcar Era,* takes us back to the days of Seattle streetcars starting more than a century ago. In detail, it outlines the streetcars' routes, controversies, and influence on local neighborhoods, as well as the reasons for their eventual collapse. The similarities between Seattle's modern light-rail system and the city's historic streetcar lines are worth noting.

In 1896, thirteen different companies provided streetcar service in Seattle. But strong forces prevailed against the streetcars, and by the late 1930s the one remaining system, the Municipal Railway, was destitute, thus ending the early days of rail transit in Seattle. Still, the flame was never fully extinguished. Over the decades, advocates laid the groundwork for the eventual return of rail transit, this time in the form of light rail that would connect Seattle to the rest of the Puget Sound region.

The old streetcar system and the modern light-rail line both faced stinging controversy. In 1919 the city of Seattle agreed to pay $15 million to acquire the private streetcar operations. This sale price was grossly inflated and a financial burden on the city, leading to loud and sustained criticism that eventually spilled into the political arena. That backlash was one of the major roadblocks preventing Seattle from receiving voter approval of badly needed streetcar improvements. Eventually buses took over.

Eighty years later, Sound Transit experienced similar blowback when it announced, before even laying an inch of track, that its first light-rail line would be three years late and cost a billion dollars more to complete. As their predecessors had done decades earlier, rail critics argued that buses are better. Sound Transit's woes became a major issue in Seattle's 2000 mayoral campaign, and around that time at least eight entities were formed to kill light rail.

As *Seattle's Streetcar Era* shows, streetcar lines from 1890 to 1910 greatly influenced neighborhood development. Homes were built close to streetcar lines, neighborhoods were pedestrian-friendly, and nearby business districts developed around the customer traffic.

That pattern continues to this day with Sound Transit's light-rail lines. Rail transit spurs development: Witness the apartment complexes and businesses in place and growing up alongside light-rail lines and stations.

Back when a streetcar ride cost a nickel and eventually a dime, Seattle Municipal Street Railway managers faced unique challenges that included the uncertainty of public financing. A state supreme court ruling at the time prohibited the city from using taxpayer dollars to support the municipal railway unless those funds were specifically approved by voters. As a consequence, financing Seattle's streetcar system became dire, leading managers to institute drastic cost-cutting measures. As streetcars deteriorated, public support wavered.

While the old streetcar system was unable to hold on, Seattle's modern light-rail system survived, thanks in part to its leadership. When it comes to major transit projects, it matters who is in charge.

Sound Transit survived its early near-fatal mistakes through a new leadership team led by Joni Earl. Her management style required tackling tough issues head-on with openness and resolve. Trust and respect for the agency eventually solidified. As a result, the first light-rail lines were built, with many more miles on the way.

Under Earl's watch, the agency grew from 261 employees to more than 700. Ridership on its trains and buses grew rapidly.

Today, light rail in Seattle carries the torch that streetcars lit more than a century ago.

Bob Wodnik served as Sound Transit's senior communications specialist from 1999 to 2017. He was a reporter and columnist for the *Everett Herald* and is author of two WSU Press books, *Back on Track: Sound Transit's Fight to Save Light Rail* (2019) and *Captured Honor: POW Survival in the Philippines and Japan* (2003).

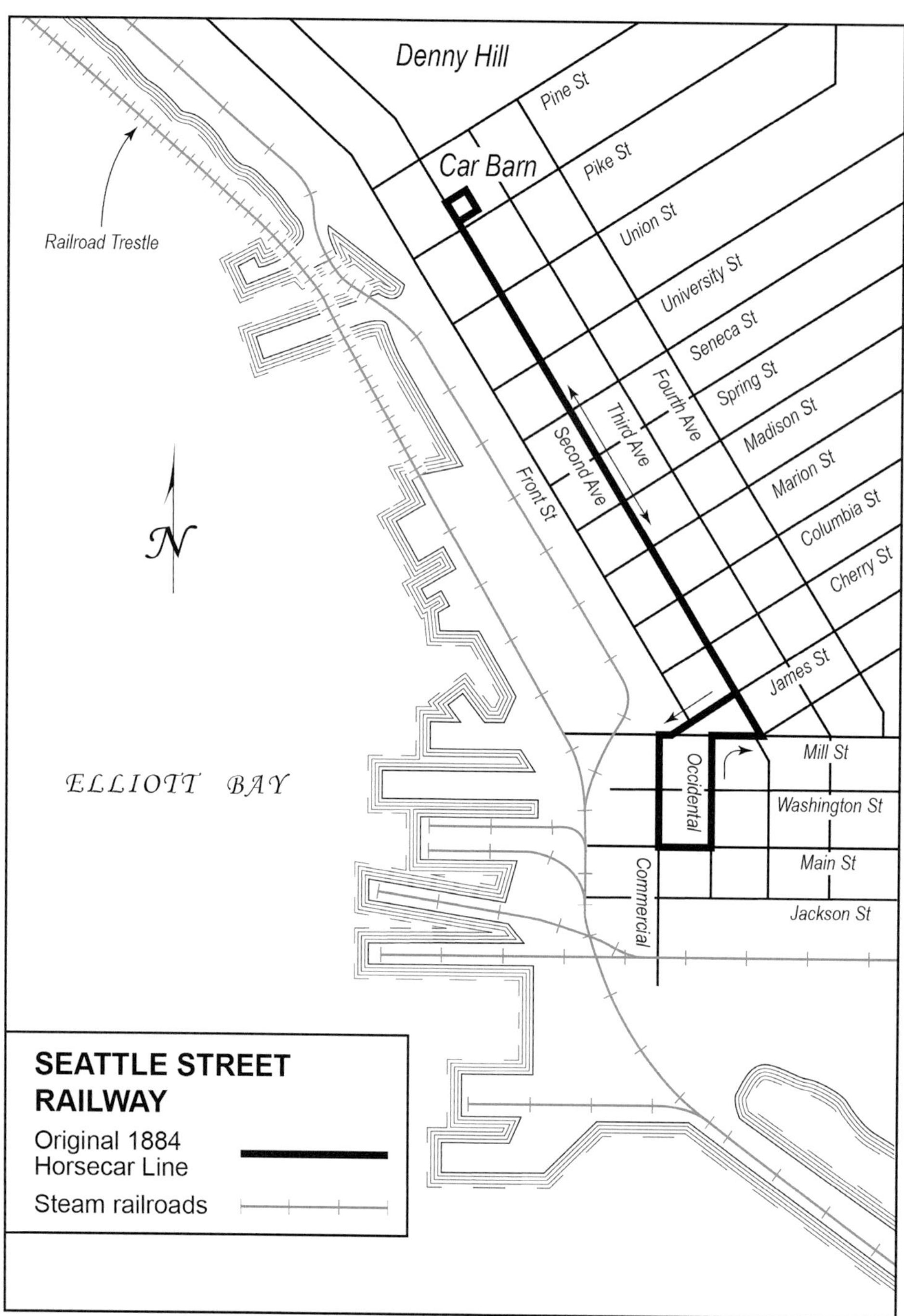

Map of Seattle Street Railway: Original 1884 horsecar line. *Map by Dave Cooley.*

Streetcars for Profit:
Privately Owned Streetcar Companies

A streetcar, according to *Webster's Dictionary of the English Language*, is "a public passenger car running on rails set in the street." Under this broad definition, a streetcar can be a rail vehicle powered by horses, electricity, or even moving underground cables. Other terms are often used for streetcars. They are sometimes called trams in Great Britain and trolleys in the United States, the latter referring to the trolley poles mounted on top of electric streetcars. Whatever term is used, the important point is that streetcars were the first widespread form of mass transportation in American cities. During the late nineteenth century and the early twentieth century, city streetcars carried more people and had greater influence on urban development than any other form of transportation.

Seattle's first streetcar lines were built by private companies, chartered under franchises issued by the city, that set the routes to be built and authorized the use of street right-of-way. Increased real estate values were frequently the primary motivation for these investments, with profits from streetcar operations as a side benefit. Seattle's first streetcar line, using streetcars pulled by horses, opened in 1884 as the city's land area started to expand beyond close-in walking distance. Streetcars pulled by underground moving cables (cable cars) began service in 1888, followed the next year by electric cars that received their power from overhead trolley wires. Electric-powered streetcars quickly became the favored mode for new lines, and by 1896 no less than thirteen private companies were operating street railways in Seattle. Between 1899 and 1907 the Seattle Electric Company, a subsidiary of utility conglomerate Stone & Webster, consolidated most of the separate companies. The city of Seattle eventually purchased the Seattle Electric system and combined it with the comparatively tiny Seattle Municipal Street Railway, creating a large, city-wide, publicly owned streetcar network. An overview of the early privately owned street railways helps to understand the challenges facing the Seattle Municipal Street Railway in later years.

The First Streetcar Line: Horse Power

Between 1880 and 1890, Seattle experienced tremendous growth, with the number of city residents increasing from 3,500 to 42,000. As the city's population grew, its geographical area expanded as well. Steep hills to the east and shorelines on the west and south restricted the supply of easily developable land, so the city initially expanded northward toward Lake Union, creating a long, narrow corridor that made an ideal route for public transportation.

Frank Osgood, who arrived in Seattle from Boston in early 1883, recognized that the rapid development of the city made it a prime candidate for a street railway, similar to lines in other U.S. cities he had visited. In the 1880s, most American street railways used horses to pull small, lightweight passenger cars. The cars ran on rails to reduce friction, which allowed the horse to pull a larger, heavier vehicle than it ordinarily could and also provided a smoother ride in an era when most city streets were unpaved.

Osgood joined forces with Judge Thomas Burke, who, along with David Denny and George Kinnear, held a city franchise for a proposed streetcar line on First Avenue. As a lawyer and businessman, Burke was instrumental in changing Seattle from a small frontier town to a major metropolitan center. His interests, in addition to street railways, included real estate, shipping, steam railroads, and mining. While Osgood was interested in the street railway solely as a way to earn profits by transporting people, Burke and his other business partners saw greater potential in increasing the value of the real estate they owned along the proposed route. Burke's approach was a common theme of Seattle's street railway financing and development over the following three decades.[1]

In early 1884, Osgood incorporated the Seattle Street Railway Company to build and operate the city's first streetcar line on First Avenue, then called Front Street. Opposition from Front Street merchants resulted in a change to the franchise authorizing the line to be

Seattle Street Railway horsecar in front of carbarn at Second Avenue and Pike Street, 1884. *PNRA photo WWWASMR-DWNTN-127.*

built on Second Avenue instead. Construction started on June 1, 1884, and the line was completed between Pioneer Square and Second Avenue and Pike Street by September 23. (See map of Seattle Street Railway.) The carbarn, originally housing four cars and twenty horses, was located on the northeast corner of Second and Pike.

Within two years of the completion of the initial line, two branches were built from the carbarn. One branch operated west on Pike to First Avenue, then north on First as far as Bell Street. The second branch, completed in early 1886, ran from Pike to the south end of Lake Union, where it connected with steamers to various points on the lake. The Seattle Street Railway was the first streetcar line in Washington Territory and a symbol of the city's rising prominence as the center of commerce on Puget Sound. When representatives of the Northern Pacific Railway visited Seattle in late 1884, Seattle mayor John Leary took them for a quick tour of the city in a buggy. "Every time I came near your tracks," Leary is reported to have said to Osgood, "I whipped up the horses and gave these fellows an awful bump, always remarking as I did so, 'By the way, you will notice that we're putting in a streetcar line.'"[2]

The First "Trolleys": Electric Streetcars

While the Seattle Street Railway was considered successful, Osgood was dismayed that it was necessary to use two horses to pull the cars, not just one as originally planned. This increased operating costs significantly and made the company only marginally profitable. Intrigued by the possibilities of electricity, Osgood read everything he could find on electric propulsion, a technology that was largely experimental in the mid-1880s. In 1888 he followed the development of Frank J. Sprague's pioneering electric streetcar line in Richmond, Virginia, which pushed the concept out of the experimental stage and into the mainstream. Sprague's system included features that would become standard on streetcars for decades to come: electric motors geared directly to the drive axle, a trolley pole kept in constant contact with the overhead power wire with spring tension, and a rotating base on the roof that allowed the trolley pole to follow the overhead wire on curves or anywhere where it wasn't directly above the center of the track. Wheels and axles were mounted on a rugged metal frame, called a truck, that supported the car and swiveled around curves. Small streetcars with seats for up to about twenty-five people were mounted on a single truck with four wheels; by the mid-1890s, double-truck cars with seats for up to fifty people were available, providing a street railway vehicle with unparalleled capacity and efficiency.[3]

Osgood convinced Burke and his other business partners that electric propulsion was the future of street railways in Seattle. He combined forces with L. H. Griffith in 1888 to form a new firm, the Seattle Electric Railway and Power Company, which would absorb the assets of the Seattle Street Railway. The new company constructed a power plant at the foot of Pike Street with a steam engine turning a Thomson-Houston generator, followed by construction of a new carbarn at Fifth Avenue and Pine Street. Five single-truck electric cars built by J. G. Brill were purchased. Trolley wire was strung over the horsecar tracks from Pioneer Square to Lake Union, and Seattle's first electric streetcar service started on March 31, 1889.

Not long after electric service began, L. H. Griffith bought out the holdings of the other company directors, including Osgood. Griffith was more interested in using street railways to enhance real estate development and did not share Osgood's view that streetcars could stand alone as a profitable enterprise with careful planning and good management. Griffith's approach resulted in many lightly used and duplicative lines being constructed during the 1890s.

Cable Cars: Seattle's Hill Climbers

Streetcars powered by a moving underground cable came into widespread use in American cities following Andrew Hallidie's successful 1873 Clay Street installation in San Francisco. The basics of a cable car system consisted of a moving wire rope running continuously in an underground conduit beneath the street, powered by a stationary steam engine or electric motor at a central powerhouse. Cable cars ran on standard or narrow-gauge track and were larger and heavier than horsecars. A "grip" attached to the car reached down through a slot into the conduit and could be adjusted by the operator to take full hold of the cable and thus move the car at the cable's typical speed of ten miles per hour. The grip provided a complete range from full release to full hold, allowing the operator to adjust the car's velocity based on traffic conditions. Cable cars were excellent at climbing and descending steep hills, which made them ideal for Seattle's rugged topography. Hillside properties previously deemed inaccessible became prized building lots with the opening of cable lines. But the first cost of developing a cable system was enormous, and ridership needed to be very high to offset the expense of maintaining a complex set of gears, flywheels, pulleys, sheaves, and other moving parts. The dust jacket copy of George Hilton's early-1970s work, *The Cable Car in America*, put it succinctly: "The cable car may have been the best thing around in the mid-1880s, but the best was none too good. Cable traction was expensive, inflexible and dangerous, economic only because the stationary steam engine that propelled the unwieldy system was so marvelously more efficient than the horse."[4]

But this view was not universally shared in 1888, when electric traction was in its infancy and cable cars had been running for some time in San Francisco and twenty-seven other U.S. cities. Entrepreneurs in Seattle were ready to invest in the proven, if awkward and

Yesler cable car loading passengers at Second Avenue and Yesler, circa 1900. *PNRA photo WWASMR-YE-033.*

Looking east on Madison Street from Western Avenue with five Madison cable cars in view, circa 1900. *PNRA photo WWASMR-MA-002 (Museum of History and Industry collection).*

expensive, cable technology. These five companies started the cable car era in Seattle:

Seattle City Railway: On September 29, 1888, passenger service began on Seattle's first cable line, which operated as a large one-way loop from Pioneer Square to Lake Washington via Yesler Way, then south along the lakeshore to Jackson Street, where the line turned west and returned to Pioneer Square. Originally built by and for the Seattle Construction Company, the three-foot-gauge line changed hands twice before being incorporated as the Seattle City Railway in late 1890.

Madison Street Cable Railway Company: The success of the Yesler line inspired investors to develop other cable lines serving Seattle's hilly neighborhoods. The Madison Street Cable Railway Company completed its initial line on Madison from the central waterfront to Twenty-Third Avenue in April 1890. By June 1891 it was extended east to Madison Park and Lake Washington.

West Seattle Cable Railway: The West Seattle Cable Railway opened in September 1890 to connect the Admiral District with a ferry to downtown Seattle on Harbor Avenue. The most short-lived of the cable lines, the company ceased operations in August 1897.

Front Street Cable Railway: Initially running from Pioneer Square to Belltown on what later was called First Avenue, the Front Street Cable Railway was extended to the top of Queen Anne

West Seattle Cable Railway car #4 next to carbarn and powerhouse, circa 1895. *PNRA photo WWASMR-WS-002 (Museum of History and Industry collection).*

First Avenue Cable Railway car #12 climbing Denny Hill on Second Avenue northbound between Pine and Stewart Streets, circa 1899. *PNRA photo WWASMR-FR-002.*

James Street open cable car #60 eastbound at Sixth Avenue, September 1903. *PNRA photo WWASMR-JA-013.*

Hill in March 1891, climbing a steep 18 percent grade on Queen Anne Avenue to reach Highland Drive.

Union Trunk Line: The Union Trunk Line opened a short but steep cable railway on James Street in 1891, running from Pioneer Square to Broadway.

As testimony to cable traction's ability to climb steep hills, three Seattle cable car lines—Yesler, Madison, and James Street—survived until 1940, after cable cars had been abandoned in every other American city except San Francisco.

Electric Streetcar Boom: The Early 1890s

The cable lines, with their complex infrastructure and high construction and maintenance costs, were limited to relatively short, high-ridership corridors on the steep hills close to downtown. Constructing new electric street railways required much less capital and could be built relatively quickly into developing residential areas several miles from the city center.

Seattle's explosive population growth continued into the early 1890s, and the pressure to accommodate new residents led to real estate development in areas that were then on the outskirts of the city, including Ballard, Phinney Ridge, Green Lake, Rainier Valley, and Georgetown. In 1895 the University of Washington, in a bold move to acquire more space, relocated its campus from downtown to a small settlement north of Portage Bay called Brooklyn (now the University District). Few of these areas could be developed as residential neighborhoods without adequate public transportation. To meet this need, seven new electric street railway companies were organized as the decade of the 1890s opened:

West Street and North End Electric Railway: This company opened an electric line between Pioneer Square, Interbay, and downtown Ballard in November 1890, when Ballard was a separate city from Seattle. The "West Street" in the title referred to today's Western Avenue, which the line used between Yesler and Denny Way. Judge Thomas Burke and his financial partner David Gilman were the major investors.

Seattle Electric Railway and Power Company: This company, which pioneered Seattle's first electric railway in 1889, extended its track from South Lake Union

Green Lake streetcar #354 at First Avenue and Yesler, circa 1902. *PNRA photo WWASMR-20-028.*

Woodland Park Electric Railway car, circa 1890. *PNRA photo WWASMR-20-051.*

to Fremont and Green Lake in 1891, creating one of Seattle's most scenic streetcar rides. Portions of the line paralleling Westlake Avenue were initially built on pilings over Lake Union.

Woodland Park Electric Railway: Guy Phinney, a major property owner in north Seattle, organized the Woodland Park Electric Railway in 1890 and began operating a short streetcar line between Woodland Park and Fremont the following year.

Rainier Power and Railway Company: Despite its name, this company had no connection with the Rainier Valley. David Denny, younger brother of Seattle founder Arthur Denny, was a major investor in the line, which connected downtown with Eastlake, Latona, Brooklyn, and Ravenna Park. The railway opened in stages between 1891 and 1892, but Denny and the company's other investors suffered large financial losses resulting from the Panic of 1893 and slow residential development in the areas served by the line. The company was reorganized as the Third Street and Suburban Railway in 1895.

David T. Denny. *Courtesy of the Seattle Municipal Archives, item 175313.*

The Union Trunk Line: Following completion of Union Trunk Line's James Street cable line in 1890, the company constructed four electric car lines: North Broadway, Madrona Park, Beacon Hill, and Rainier Heights. Connecting with the cable car terminus at Broadway and James, the electric lines opened between 1891 and 1893. All of the company's tracks were built to the narrow gauge of three feet six inches.

Rainier Avenue Electric Railway: Seattle's southeast neighborhoods were served by an early electric interurban line, the Rainier Avenue Electric Railway. Frank Osgood, who had managed the development of Seattle's 1884 horsecar start-up, furnished and supervised the installation of the electrical equipment for the company and later became general manager. By late 1890, service was operating between Pioneer Square and Columbia City. The

Employees gather by James Street cable car #70 at the Broadway and James Street carbarn, circa 1901. *PNRA photo WWASMR-JA-018.*

Seattle and Renton Railway open car #18 in Columbia City, circa 1899. *PNRA photo WWASRV-056.*

Grant Street Electric Railway narrow-gauge car #12 in Georgetown, circa 1895. *PNRA photo WWASMR-06-064.*

line became a true "interurban" in 1896 when track was extended to downtown Renton, and the name was then changed to the Seattle and Renton Railway. This company became the longest surviving independent streetcar company in Seattle, operating until 1937.[5]

Grant Street Electric Railway: The Grant Street Electric Railway opened in January 1892 between Pioneer Square, Georgetown, and South Park. Originally intended to be the first leg of an interurban to Tacoma, the line ran on Grant Street (today's Airport Way), which skirted the base of Beacon Hill. The company's generating plant in Georgetown was large enough to provide excess power that was sold to other commercial enterprises in the vicinity—a sign of things to come at other street railway properties. The Grant Street Electric Railway used the Union Trunk Line's narrow track gauge of three feet six inches.

The Panic of 1893 and Early Efforts to Consolidate

The starting up of new street railway companies came to a halt during the Panic of 1893, a relatively short but severe economic depression that had a profound impact on business ventures throughout the United States. Street railways in Seattle were particularly hard-hit, as they had been financed with the expectation of steadily increasing ridership and escalating real estate values. Few companies escaped bankruptcy, foreclosure, or both, although only one company was shut down and liquidated. (For example, Denny's Rainier Power and Railway Company went into receivership during the Panic of 1893 and was reorganized as the Third Street and Suburban Railway in 1895. It continued to struggle financially until absorbed by the Seattle Electric conglomerate in 1899.) As the economy slowly recovered, it became clear that there were serious flaws in the fundamental process of how Seattle's street railways had been planned, constructed, and operated.

First off, many of the lines had been built cheaply and hurriedly, with poor-quality rail, inadequate power supplies, and long sections of single track that could be used in only one direction at a time. In his biography of Judge Thomas Burke, Robert C. Nesbit described how Burke's West Street and North End Railway sold its original power generating building in Interbay to raise cash and moved the generator to the basement of the Burke Building at Second and Marion. In addition to powering the streetcars, the generator also supplied power for the building. If too many streetcars accelerated on the line at the same time, the lights in the building would dim and the elevators would slow to a crawl.[6]

In the rush to be the first to reach growing neighborhoods, individual companies often built duplicative lines that were too close to each other, diluting the passenger traffic. For example, in 1896 the lower Queen Anne area had parallel streetcar lines on First Avenue West, First Avenue North, and Second Avenue North, running one or

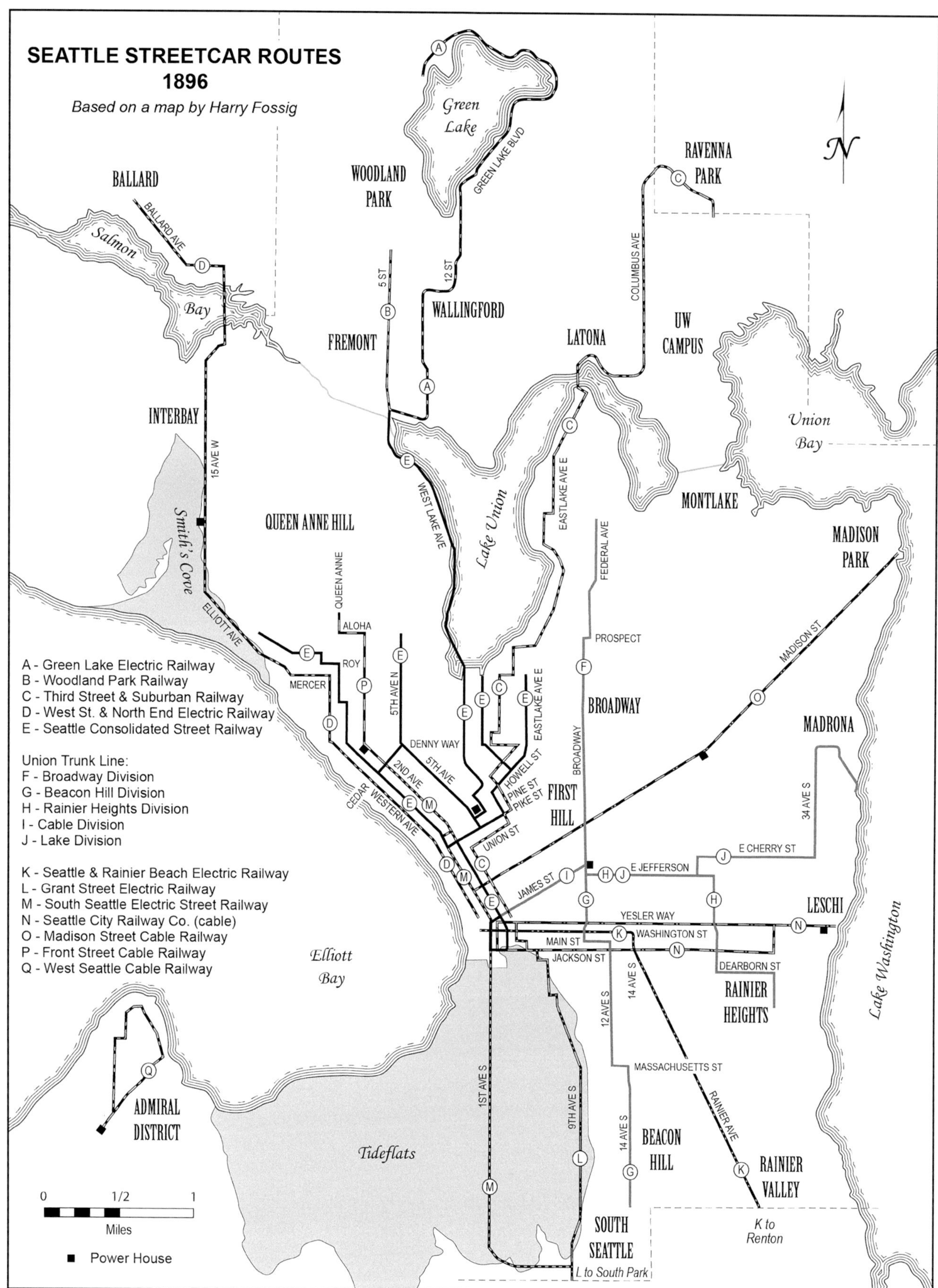

Map of independent streetcar lines in Seattle, 1896. *Map by Dave Cooley.*

two blocks apart. Similarly, the South Lake Union/Cascade neighborhood had parallel lines on Fairview, Pontius, and Eastlake Avenues, also just a block or two apart. It was clear that there was no comprehensive, logical plan for Seattle's street railway system based on need and ridership potential.

One obvious flaw was that the proliferation of small, independent companies failed to achieve economies of scale. Each company had its own powerhouse, carbarn, and car fleet, and four companies used narrow-gauge track, which ruled out streetcar interchangeability with the standard-gauge lines. There was also duplication of overhead, administrative, and maintenance functions.

Efforts to consolidate began in mid-1893 with a proposal to merge several of the cable and electric lines. By that time David Denny had assumed control of the Seattle Electric Railway and Power Company, the Green Lake Electric Railway Company, the Front Street Cable Railway Company, and the Rainier Power and Railway Company. These companies operated a combined total of thirty-three miles of electric lines and ten miles of cable lines. But a disagreement among the stockholders kept any acquisition or merger plans from moving forward, and the companies maintained their separate corporate identities and operation until the Boston engineering firm of Stone & Webster entered the picture in 1899.

STONE & WEBSTER

Charles Stone and Edwin Webster met in 1884 while both were studying electrical engineering at the Massachusetts Institute of Technology. They formed a consulting firm in 1890, providing technical services and management advice for the rapidly developing electric lighting and street railway industries. Stone & Webster not only had insight in developing and managing utilities, but they also possessed keen intuition for business investment. They were particularly interested in Washington State, with its large hydroelectric power potential and rapidly growing urban population. Appointing a respected Seattle banker, Jacob Furth, as their agent, they formed the Seattle Electric Company in 1899 and obtained a thirty-five-year franchise to purchase and combine the operations of six existing street railways: Grant Street Railway, Union Trunk Line, Third Street and Suburban Railway, Front Street Cable Railway, Madison Street Cable Railway, and Seattle Traction Company. Furth, who was named president of Seattle Electric in 1902, said that Stone & Webster would invest $1 million to make needed improvements and integrate the operations of the separate companies. But that wasn't all. Later that same year, Stone & Webster purchased several privately owned gas and electric utilities in Seattle and folded them into Seattle Electric, essentially

Seattle Traction Company car #4 at Third Avenue and Jefferson Street in 1901, shortly after STC had been absorbed by Seattle Electric. *PNRA photo WWAST-16-032.*

creating a near monopoly in both the street railway and energy utilities. Major financing came from the New York investment banking firms Lee, Higginson & Company and Kidder Peabody.[7]

The "invasion" of East Coast capital did not sit well with many Seattle residents, some of whom argued for municipal ownership of all utilities, including street railways. They particularly resented the fact that major decisions affecting Seattle would be made in private by wealthy men in faraway Boston. But Furth and other respected local leaders, including Judge Burke, made the case that only outside capital could bring in the resources needed to turn the local companies around.

The Seattle Electric Company continued its street railway consolidation program over the next eight years. All of the independent street railways in Seattle were acquired except the Seattle, Renton and Southern (later renamed the Seattle and Rainier Valley Railway), which remained a separate operation. In 1907 the electric-powered West Seattle Municipal Railway, successor to the short-lived West Seattle Cable Railway Company, became the last independent line purchased by Seattle Electric.

Big Improvements and New Lines

After acquiring most of the independent companies, Stone & Webster, acting through its local subsidiary, Seattle Electric, made good on its commitment to improve and expand Seattle's streetcar system. Virtually all lines received double track, heavier rail, and better roadbeds. Single track was confined to sections close to the end of the line or short shuttle routes running with only one or two cars. Extensions into developing neighborhoods were constructed together with the abandonment of closely spaced lines that duplicated each other. Small, single-truck streetcars with limited capacity were replaced with larger, more comfortable double-truck cars. As the city's principal electric utility, the Seattle Electric Company shifted away from generating plants that existed solely for streetcar power and built new plants that were interconnected and supplied power to multiple users. This had the side benefit of improving the reliability of the streetcar power supply.

Seattle Electric also made major investments to continue three of the remaining cable car lines. Between 1899 and 1900, the Yesler–Jackson line was completely reconfigured; the Yesler Way segment was double-tracked and made two-way, and a new powerhouse was constructed on Lake Washington near Leschi Park. The Jackson Street segment was converted to an electric streetcar line following a major regrading of the street to reduce steep grades. In 1910 the Madison cable line was truncated at Fourteenth Avenue, with the section east of Fourteenth converted to electric operation. But the remaining cable track was extensively rebuilt, and a new powerhouse near Broadway replaced the original installation at Twenty-Second Avenue and Madison. The short James Street line received new double-truck, home-built cars, and the powerhouse was converted from steam to electricity in 1900.

In 1902 the former Front Street Cable Railway line from Pioneer Square to Queen Anne Hill was extensively rebuilt into an unusual combination of cable and electric streetcar operation. The entire line was electrified, but the 18 percent grade on Queen Anne Avenue was too steep

Looking east on Madison Street toward Lake Washington with two cable cars in the distance, circa 1891. *PNRA photo WWASMR-MA-006 (Dan Kerlee collection).*

for conventional electric streetcars. The solution was to equip the segment between Lee Street and Roy Street with a "counterbalance" cable system. Shallow tunnels were constructed beneath each of the two tracks on the hill. A heavy concrete-filled railcar ran on its own tracks through each of the tunnels, out of sight. This counterbalance car pulled a cable that assisted conventional electric streetcars climbing and descending the hill using a hook that protruded from a slot between the rails. In outward appearance the track and center slot looked like a conventional cable car line, except the cable was powered by gravity instead of a steam engine or electric motor at a central powerhouse. Since the underground counterbalance cars were almost the same weight as the streetcars, the electric cars moved up the hill effortlessly. Conversely, the downhill trip was made much safer, since the streetcar was pulling the counterbalance car in the uphill direction, minimizing the use of the regular service brakes. It was an ingenious idea and less costly to operate than a conventional cable line. Amazingly, the counterbalance system would survive until August 1940, less than a year before all rail operations ceased.

The Seattle Electric Company, with financing from parent Stone & Webster, continued to build new streetcar

Car #320 on Queen Anne counterbalance line, 1908. Note the crossover tracks and center slot for the cable that assisted cars up and down the hill. *PNRA photo WWASMR-026-019.*

lines and extensions of existing lines through the first decade of the twentieth century. With tracks already in place between downtown and Fremont, the company developed a network of North End lines converging on the Fremont business district. These included the Phinney–Greenwood line, the West Woodland line, and two lines serving Wallingford, one of which continued east to the University District. Seattle Electric also used a combination of existing and new tracks to connect Fremont with Ballard and Ballard Beach. These new lines joined the Green Lake line, which had been in operation since 1891, making Fremont a major hub of the growing streetcar network.

Magnolia Bluff received its first and only streetcar service in 1905 when the Seattle Electric Company opened the Fort Lawton line. It branched off the old West Street and North End Railway at Fifteenth Avenue West and Dravus Street, then continued west on Dravus and around the north end of the bluff, entering the fort on Government Way.

Direct streetcar service between downtown Seattle and West Seattle began on January 4, 1907, with the opening of the Fauntleroy line, followed later that year by the Alki Point line, which shared the Fauntleroy line's track between downtown and Youngstown. About this time Seattle Electric extended the former West Seattle Municipal Railway (now electrically operated) south from the Admiral District to join with the Fauntleroy line at California Avenue and Alaska Street. The neighborhood around this intersection soon became known as "the Junction," a name still in widespread use today.

Seattle's South End was not overlooked in the rebuilding and extension plans. The former narrow-gauge Grant Street Electric Railway, which had inaugurated streetcar service to Georgetown and South Park, was designated the South Seattle line when the Seattle Electric Company took over and converted it to standard gauge. A segment of the South Seattle line through Georgetown was used by the Puget Sound Electric Railway interurban that ran between Seattle and Tacoma.

In 1909, Seattle hosted a world's fair, the Alaska-Yukon-Pacific Exposition (A-Y-P), which took place on the University of Washington campus. To prepare for the exposition, the Seattle Electric Company made major service improvements to its two existing routes between downtown Seattle and the University District, the Broadway and Eastlake lines. The company also initiated a new service that started on Jackson Street near the railroad depots, operated east on Jackson, then north on Twenty-Third and Twenty-Fourth Avenues to the south entrance of the A-Y-P grounds. Millions of passengers used Seattle Electric streetcars to reach the A-Y-P during the six-month fair.

The expanded system required additional space for storing and maintaining the streetcar fleet, and Seattle

Fauntleroy car #604 at the Endolyne loop, Forty-Fifth Avenue SW and SW Roxbury Street, 1910. *PNRA photo WWASMR-02-054.*

Electric followed up with construction of three new permanent carbarns: North Seattle, at Fifth Avenue North and Mercer Street (1905); Georgetown, at Airport Way and South Hardy Street (1906); and Fremont, at Phinney Avenue and North Thirty-Fourth Street (1909). The company also built a "temporary" wooden carbarn at Fourteenth Avenue and Jefferson Street to support increased service during the A-Y-P. The Jefferson Street carbarn continued to operate until the end of rail service, and for decades afterward it was used as a trolley coach facility. Georgetown was designed for heavy maintenance and overhauls, and handled streetcars brought in from around the system.

Seattle Electric's tenure as the local streetcar operator coincided with major man-made changes to the city's topography. The regrading of Seattle's hills began during the 1890s and continued into the early 1930s, resulting in many temporary arrangements to keep streetcar service going, particularly in the Denny Hill area and on the cable lines as they approached downtown. Construction of the Lake Washington Ship Canal began in 1910 and resulted in temporary bridges at Ballard, Fremont, and Latona, complete with temporary streetcar tracks. Tracks originally built on pilings over water—including those on Grant Street/ Airport Way, along Alki Avenue near Duwamish Head, and on the west shore of Lake Union—were relaid on solid ground as large areas of the city's waterways were filled in.[8]

Political boundaries in Seattle were also changing dramatically as Seattle annexed other jurisdictions and unincorporated areas. Between 1900 and 1910 the area of the city doubled through annexation, from 34 to 71 square miles, and the population increased from 81,000 to 237,000. Ballard, Georgetown, South Park, and West Seattle, which had been separate cities, became part of the city of Seattle, as did a number of smaller unincorporated areas. The major motivation for the annexation movement was adequate and reliable water supplies, but other factors, including Seattle's ability to provide needed bridges, streets, and other infrastructure, were also important considerations.

New and existing streetcar lines continued to figure prominently in the city's development during the first decade of the century. Streetcars provided both mobility and stability, so investment flowed into residential areas within easy walking distance of frequent service. Compared with earlier eras of Seattle's growth, these "streetcar suburbs" were well planned and included public infrastructure most people take for granted today, such as streetlights, sidewalks, and paved streets. Many of Seattle's parks and boulevards were established during the decade of 1900 to 1910, offering additional amenities for the new neighborhoods. The quality of housing

Fremont carbarn viewed from Lake Washington Ship Canal with tug *Lumberman* in foreground, 1919. *PNRA photo WWASMR-019-035.*

construction improved and homes displayed a variety of interesting architectural styles, including Queen Anne Revival, Craftsman, Tudor Revival, Colonial, and Classic Box. The multifamily apartment building became a fixture in many Seattle neighborhoods, increasing population density and generating additional streetcar riders.

Streetcars also provided the catalyst for the development of many Seattle neighborhood business districts. Small businesses, like grocery stores, bakeries, drugstores, and hardware stores, that provided basic household needs tended to cluster together at streetcar terminals and junctions. Streetcars provided access to these commercial enterprises but also generated foot traffic, which was important for impulse buying. The largest neighborhood business districts were those where multiple streetcar lines converged, including downtown Ballard, the University District, Fremont, the East Madison Street district, and West Seattle Junction.

Downtown Seattle was by far the largest business district that benefited from the streetcar expansion. The streetcar network focused on downtown, since it was the most important activity center in the region: a center of government, finance, corporate offices, retail, and entertainment.

Seattle Electric Company's streetcar ridership totaled 103 million passengers in 1910, meaning that, on average, every man, woman, and child in Seattle boarded a streetcar 435 times that year. The company's expansion and improvement program coincided with the largest one-decade population increase in the city's history. Almost any place in the city worth visiting was accessible by a nickel streetcar ride. The company had a near monopoly on streetcar service in Seattle. Travel by private motor vehicle was just beginning, but streetcar managers took little heed, as automobiles represented a tiny percentage of total traffic. Apart from the horse and buggy, the streetcars had little competition.

Route 7 car passing underneath temporary ceremonial arch northbound at First Avenue and Columbia Street, 1902. *PNRA photo WWASMR-07-022.*

Streetcars for the People:
Municipal Ownership

The first years of the new century saw a continuation of the Progressive movement, a period of widespread social activism and political reform across the United States. One of the main objectives of the movement was addressing the excesses of capitalism, including economic inequality, excessive corporate power, worker exploitation, and political corruption. Shortly after taking office in 1901, President Theodore Roosevelt shocked his Republican Party colleagues by announcing he would target the wealth and power of big business. In 1902 he brought legal action against the Northern Securities Company, a railroad trust that had gained a hammerlock on rail transportation between Chicago and Seattle. In attacking Northern Securities, Roosevelt took on four of the country's most powerful men: oilman John D. Rockefeller, railroad barons James J. Hill and Edward H. Harriman, and investment banker J. P. Morgan. The president made use of a then-little-known statute, the 1890 Sherman Anti-Trust Act, to force the breakup of Northern Securities. He followed this with lawsuits against Standard Oil, the American Tobacco Company, DuPont, the Chicago meat-packers, and some forty other trusts. All of these suits were successful at breaking up monopolies that engaged in price fixing, elimination of competition, and political kickbacks to gain power.

These and similar events produced a general uneasiness in Seattle about large, nationwide corporations and trusts. Activists were particularly concerned about public utilities, which were crucial to community growth and economic development. Public utilities were increasingly being purchased by large holding companies, which became highly profitable by spreading risk while being insulated from the responsibility of providing reliable service. On one hand, holding companies gained tremendous efficiencies and economies of scale by having exclusive franchises. On the other, they then had the ability to exploit the public with rate hikes and dictate when and where development would take place.

One reaction to the public utility issue was the establishment of state regulatory agencies. The Washington State Legislature created the Railroad Commission of Washington in 1905 to regulate railroad companies. The name was changed in 1911 to the Public Service Commission of Washington and the agency was given much broader powers, including the power to "regulate the rates, services, facilities and practices...of those engaged in the business of supplying any utility service or commodity to the public for compensation."[1] Notably, city-owned utilities were exempt from the agency's jurisdiction. The creation of the Public Service Commission spurred Stone & Webster to consolidate its various Puget Sound operations, which included local power and streetcar companies in Bellingham, Everett, and Tacoma as well as Seattle. Consolidation increased efficiency, reduced overhead, and provided a unified front in negotiations with the Public Service Commission. The new firm would be known as the Puget Sound Traction, Light and Power Company (PSTL&P), and it replaced the Seattle Electric Company as the city's principal streetcar operator on April 1, 1912.

In the meantime, advocates of public ownership were making inroads. Seattle's water supply had become a municipal function during the 1890s, and Seattle City Light was formed in 1904 to build a hydroelectric power plant at Cedar Falls, located near North Bend. The city had completed a water supply dam and reservoir at Cedar Falls in 1901, and it was obvious that it had potential as a source of inexpensive electric power. Support for the city-owned electric utility came from a variety of interests, including the Municipal Ownership League, a local business coalition that had as its goal the breaking of the electrical franchise monopoly. The Seattle Manufacturers Association contended that the city should compete with the "absentee" corporation (Stone & Webster) to drive down electric rates and improve and extend services. Seattle City Light also gained the support of organized labor, since it was a recognized union shop, while Stone & Webster did its utmost to discourage employees from organizing. Competition from City Light had the desired effect of reducing the private company's commercial rates from 20 cents to 12 cents per kilowatt hour shortly after the Cedar Falls plant came on line.

City engineer R. H. Thompson, a firm believer in municipal ownership, promoted a bond issue to raise $6 million for a new city-owned streetcar system in 1906. The proposition was fiercely opposed by *Seattle Daily Times* publisher Alden J. Blethen: "The *Times* repeatedly attacked the 'municipal ownership faddists' whose plans could jeopardize Seattle's credit with investors. On the editorial page, Blethen insisted that city control would make the streetcar system more costly and less efficient than it was under private ownership; other cities had been bankrupted by such experiments, he claimed. Blethen also had strong personal attachments in the Seattle fight. His old ally Jacob Furth was president of the Seattle Electric Company, the operator of the city's transit system."[2]

In the September 1906 election, the street railway bond issue was defeated by 1,436 votes. But the Municipal Ownership League continued its efforts to bring utilities under direct city control and to restrict the granting of franchises. Even the city's Protestant clergy championed municipal ownership as a way to control graft involving politicians and private interests. The league also advocated direct legislation as a means of limiting corporate influence on city government. This ultimately resulted in 1908 legislation requiring that city franchises be approved by referendum vote.[3]

The Municipal Railway Becomes a Reality: "Division A"

The beginnings of the Seattle Municipal Street Railway came about not as part of a carefully researched plan but through a series of random opportunities that coincided with the municipal ownership movement.

Advocates of municipal ownership on the city council looked closely at acquiring the Seattle, Renton and Southern Railway, an independent street railway company not under Seattle Electric's control and which connected Seattle with Renton via Rainier Avenue. Major improvements had been made to the line between 1907 and 1910, including construction of a more direct route into the center of downtown and the purchase of eleven new large-capacity streetcars. But the company had incurred the wrath of its riders in 1910 by proposing zone fares for longer trips, followed the next year by a decision to no longer accept Seattle Electric transfers. Municipal ownership advocates hoped that, by acquiring an existing street railway company, they could demonstrate that the city could be a good manager while providing service based on community priorities rather than profit.

In 1911, municipal ownership advocates on the city council succeeded in getting a referendum on the ballot for an $800,000 bond issue to initiate the Seattle Municipal Street Railway. This time the smaller bond issue passed easily. However, Renton residents opposed Seattle's proposed acquisition of the Seattle, Renton and Southern Railway and apparently no one had talked to the company about price. Company management, citing the improvements made to the line during the preceding five years, placed a value of $1.2 million for the property. This valuation, $400,000 higher than expected, put a halt to further discussion of acquiring the line, at least for the time being, and the Seattle, Renton and Southern remained in private hands.

The ordinance authorizing the bond issue had been broadly written to include the acquisition or construction of other street railways, so the $800,000 was set aside for "Division A," a new line that would serve the eastern and northern slopes of Queen Anne Hill. Construction started in September 1912, and Division A was completed and opened for service on May 23, 1914. Day-to-day management was assigned to the city's Department of Public Utilities, with the city council acting as the governing board.

From a ridership perspective, Division A faced major challenges. There were no free transfers between the municipal line and the private company's streetcars. From downtown, the line ran north on Third Avenue through a vacant, newly leveled part of the Denny Regrade, then zigzagged its way to Dexter Avenue to avoid the remaining sections of Denny Hill that had not yet been removed. North of Mercer Street, the steep Queen Anne hillside limited the population that could access Dexter, with side streets extending only a block or two on either side of the streetcar line. As the tracks descended down to Nickerson Street on the north side of the hill, ridership was limited by similar geographic constraints. The four-mile line ended "in the middle of nowhere" at the south end of the Fourteenth Avenue NW Bridge over Salmon Bay, requiring a transfer to PSTL&P streetcars to reach Ballard.

But Division A had several interesting technical features. The line was entirely double-track (one track in each direction) and had two trolley wires over each track, together with two parallel trolley poles on tops of the streetcars. The purpose of having twin overhead wires was to avoid the ground electrical return through the streetcar wheels and rails. Since the beginning of electric street railways, stray electric current from the wheels would seek out pathways through underground utilities and cause electrolytic damage to water, sewer, and gas pipelines. Improvements to electrical bonding between the rails addressed this problem in later years.

The city ordered twelve new double-truck streetcars to provide service on the line, built by the Cincinnati

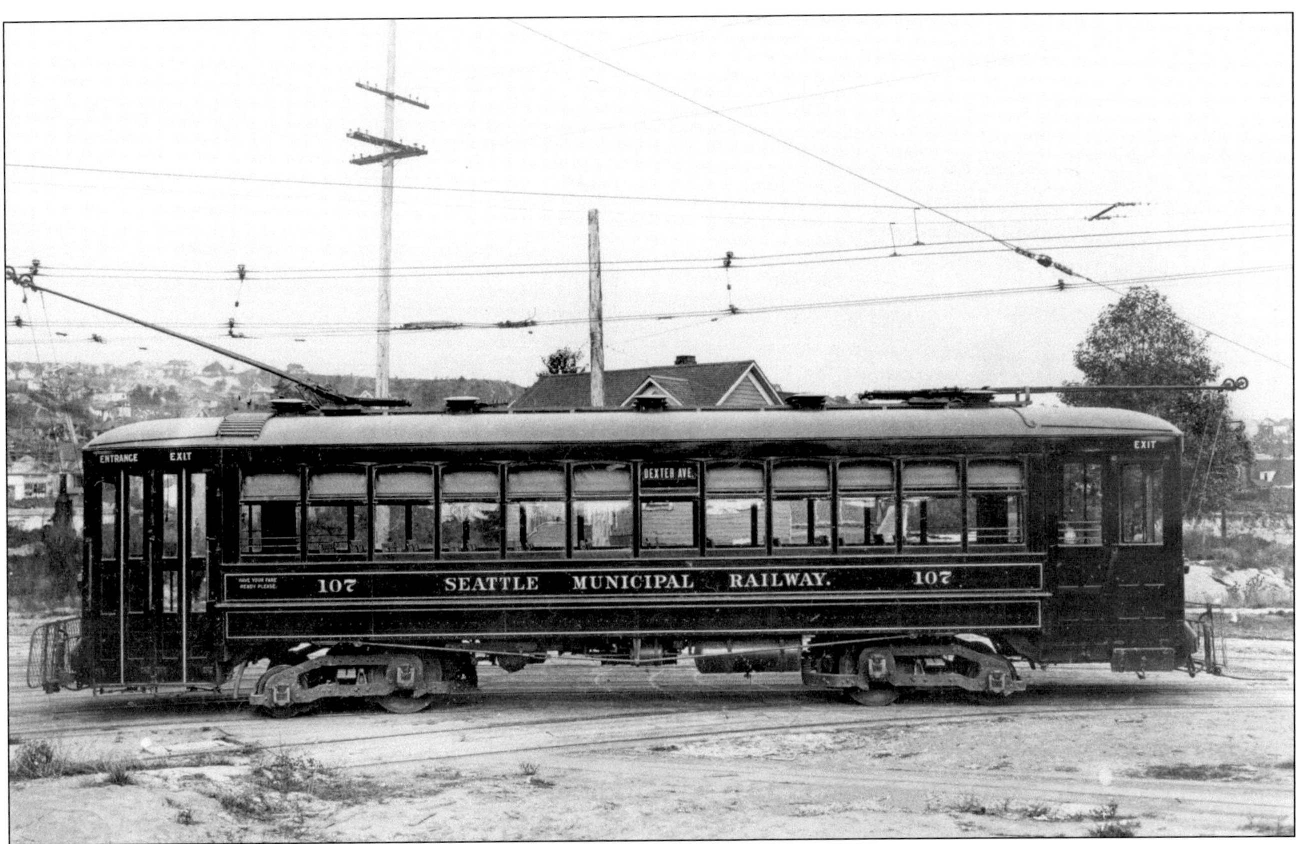

New Seattle Municipal Street Railway car #107 at Nickerson Street carbarn, 1914. *PNRA photo WWASMR-NIC-002.*

Car Company and delivered in early 1914. The cars were state-of-the-art, comfortably furnished, and equipped with multiple unit controllers so that they could be operated together as two-car trains. A small carbarn to house them was constructed on Third Avenue West just north of Nickerson Street.

DIVISION A AND THE LOYAL RAILWAY

The close relationship between real estate developers and new streetcar lines continued even after Seattle Electric consolidated most of the independent streetcar companies. One of the most colorful of the independent lines was the Loyal Railway, built by Harry Whitney Treat, a major landowner and developer in Ballard. Treat purchased beachfront land in northern Ballard as a private park and named it "Golden Gardens." To maximize the potential of his nearby properties, Treat's streetcar line connected downtown Ballard with the intersection of Thirty-Second Avenue NW and NW Eighty-Fifth Street, where a stairway was constructed down the steep hillside to the park. The new residential area near the end of the line was named Loyal Heights, after Treat's daughter Loyal.

Treat was granted a franchise from the city of Ballard for his line, and the first 1.5-mile segment opened for service on May 1, 1906. A short two-block extension on Market Street opened later that year. Base service was provided every sixty minutes with one car, with a second car added during peak demand periods. The streetcars were housed in a small carbarn at NW Eighty-Third Street and Loyal Way near the end of the line, and power came from a substation shared with the Seattle–Everett interurban, located near Fourteenth Avenue NW and NW Leary Way.

Ballard was annexed to the city of Seattle in 1907, and the Loyal Railway was purchased by the city on January 7, 1918. Shortly after, Division A was extended across the Ballard Bridge under a trackage rights agreement with Puget Sound Traction, Light and Power. At Twentieth Avenue NW and NW Market Street, municipal streetcars connected with Loyal Railway trackage, and on March 12, 1918, through streetcar service was established all the way from Loyal Heights to downtown Seattle. (See map of Division A and Loyal Railway consolidation.) The Municipal Railway finally had a line with ridership potential.[4]

DIVISION C: THE HIGHLAND PARK AND LAKE BURIEN RAILROAD

The unincorporated suburban area southwest of Seattle was ripe for development by the second decade of the twentieth century. Known as the "Highline" district to distinguish it from the low-lying Green River valley to the east, the area was largely open countryside and had very few roads. A group of nine local real estate investors recognized that convenient transportation was needed to make their properties attractive for development. They incorporated the Highland Park and Lake Burien Railroad (HP&LB) in late 1911, intent on connecting Seahurst, Burien, White Center, and Highland Park with Seattle. After obtaining franchises from the city of Seattle and King County, the company quickly proceeded to build a single-track electric line using a combination of public streets and private right-of-way. Having little experience in the street railway industry, they leased two secondhand streetcars from Puget Sound Traction, Light and Power to provide the service and contracted with the larger company to operate and maintain the line. Residential lots were advertised in local newspapers

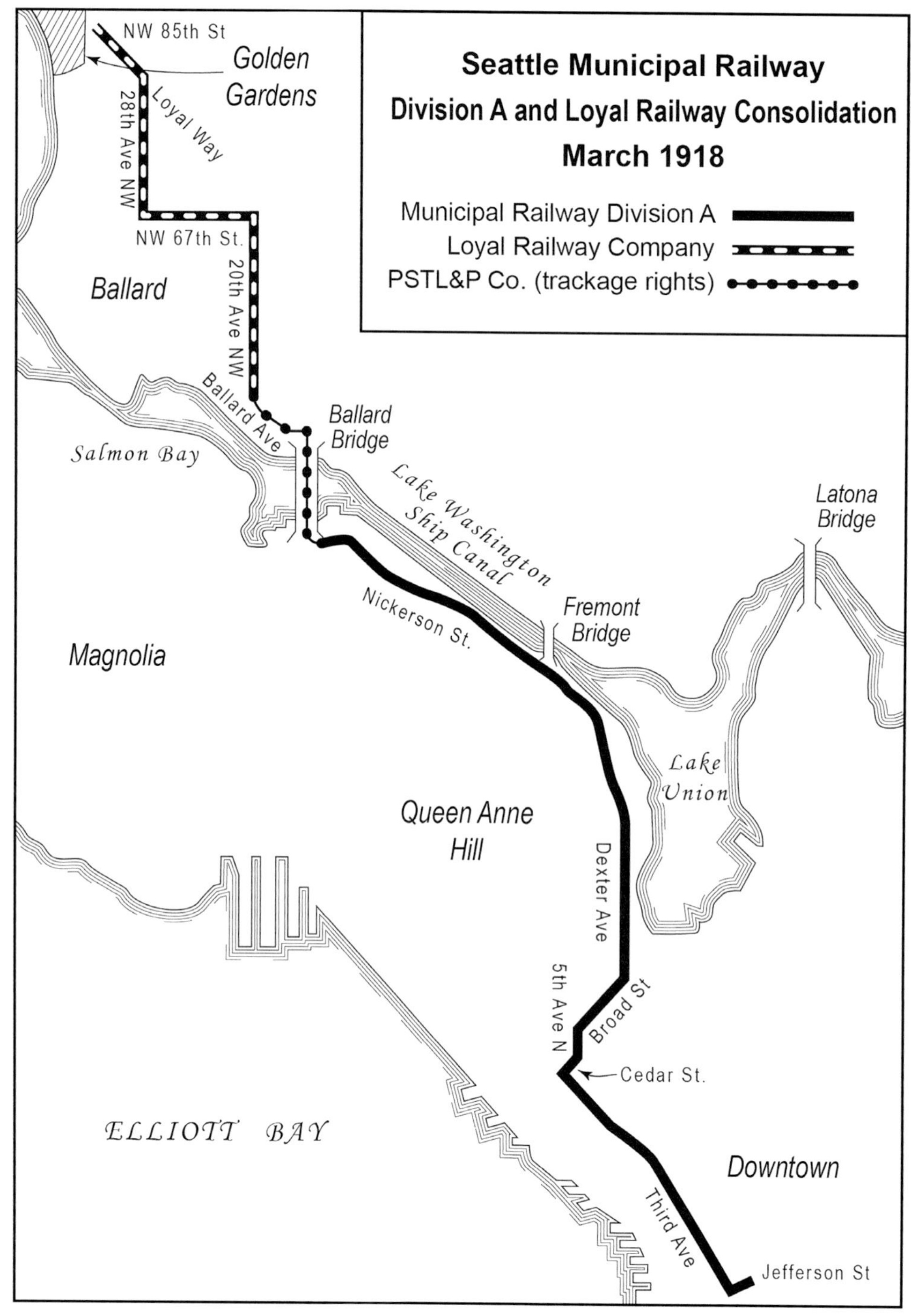

Map of Division A and Loyal Railway consolidation. *Map by Dave Cooley.*

Opening day of Highland Park and Lake Burien Railroad at Green Station with one of the original cars used on the line, 1912. *PNRA photo WWAHP-018.*

touting the accessibility of the Highline district with the new streetcar line. Significantly, it became the last new streetcar line in the Seattle area developed by real estate investors.

The Highland Park and Lake Burien Railroad started at the community of Riverside, near the west end of the Spokane Street Bridge in West Seattle. Initially, passengers transferred here to Puget Sound Traction, Light and Power Company streetcars to reach downtown Seattle. Riverside also had a connecting track with the Northern Pacific Railway, allowing freight cars to be interchanged with mainline steam railroads. From Riverside, the HP&LB headed south on West Marginal Way, then entered private right-of-way through the heavily forested West Duwamish Greenbelt to reach Highland Park. The line continued on city streets through Highland Park to the White Center business district, then headed south to Burien near Ambaum Boulevard SW and SW 152nd Street. From there, it turned west for about a mile, ending at the coastal community of Seahurst. (See map of Highland Park and Lake Burien line.) Regular service started in June 1912 on this scenic trolley ride into what was then largely undeveloped countryside.

The new line had been in operation for only a few months when service was halted on November 8, 1912. A major landslide in the West Duwamish Greenbelt between Riverside and Highland Park severely damaged almost a mile of track and trolley wire. By this time the company had been foreclosed and taken over by the contractor that built the line. The railway's new owners quickly offered to donate it to the city of Seattle on the condition that the city repair the slide damage and restore service. With proponents of municipal ownership now in the majority on the city council, the city accepted the donation in July 1913 and awarded a contract for repairs. Service was restored on May 14, 1914, just nine days before Division A opened, and the former Highland Park and Lake Burien Railroad became Division C of the Municipal Railway. (The Seattle, Renton and Southern Railway was envisioned as Division B.) The city quickly disposed of the small, single-truck streetcars that started service on the line and replaced them with new cars originally built for Division A. A small carbarn was constructed on Ninth Avenue SW in Highland Park to store and maintain the line's streetcars.

Changes at Puget Sound Traction, Light and Power Company

While the city of Seattle was developing a separate municipal streetcar system, Puget Sound Traction, Light and Power Company was shifting away from street railway investment and more toward the electric power business. Between 1912 and 1920, the Puget

Contractor repairing Highland Park and Lake Burien slide damage with Duwamish River in background, 1913. *PNRA photo WWAHP-002.*

Sound Traction, Light and Power Company acquired eight more power companies in the Puget Sound region and integrated them into their existing properties. The company constructed new 55,000-volt transmission lines to link their power plants at Snoqualmie Falls, White River, Nooksack, Electron, and Georgetown, improving the reliability of power delivery. The demand for electric power seemed almost insatiable.

In the meantime, expansion of the Seattle streetcar system slowed to a halt. The company did acquire new streetcars during this period to replace original equipment, including thirty-nine single-truck "Birney Safety Cars." These small, lightweight cars designed by Charles O. Birney, a Stone & Webster engineer, were equipped with safety devices to permit one-man operation. The city of Seattle was also impressed by the economic advantages of the Birneys. Twelve of them were purchased by the Municipal Railway in 1918, and they became the last new streetcars delivered to Seattle until the 2007 start-up of the South Lake Union line.[5]

PSTL&P president Jacob Furth died in 1914 and was replaced by Alton W. Leonard, a native New Englander who came through the Stone & Webster ranks to become a vice president in 1912. The loss of longtime Seattle resident Furth as president and his replacement with an East Coast company man seemed to confirm the worst suspicions of the press and municipal ownership supporters: "From the moment he was named president in 1914, Leonard's New England origins, combined with the fact that Stone & Webster (acting for mainly eastern stockholders) was the source of his election, were seized on by the local press as evidence that he was only the agent of 'Boston big money power trusters.'"[6]

Shortly after taking office as president, Leonard had his hands full managing both the Seattle streetcar lines and the company's electric power business. "Jitneys" started appearing on Seattle streets in 1914. They were private automobiles that cruised along streetcar lines and picked up waiting streetcar passengers for five cents. ("Jitney" was a slang term for a nickel.) By May 1915, PSTL&P spokesman A. L. Kempster estimated that jitneys were taking about 16 percent of the company's streetcar traffic. With support from the company, the city of Seattle, and labor unions, state legislation was passed later that year that allowed cities to regulate jitney routes and hours of service, and required each operator to post

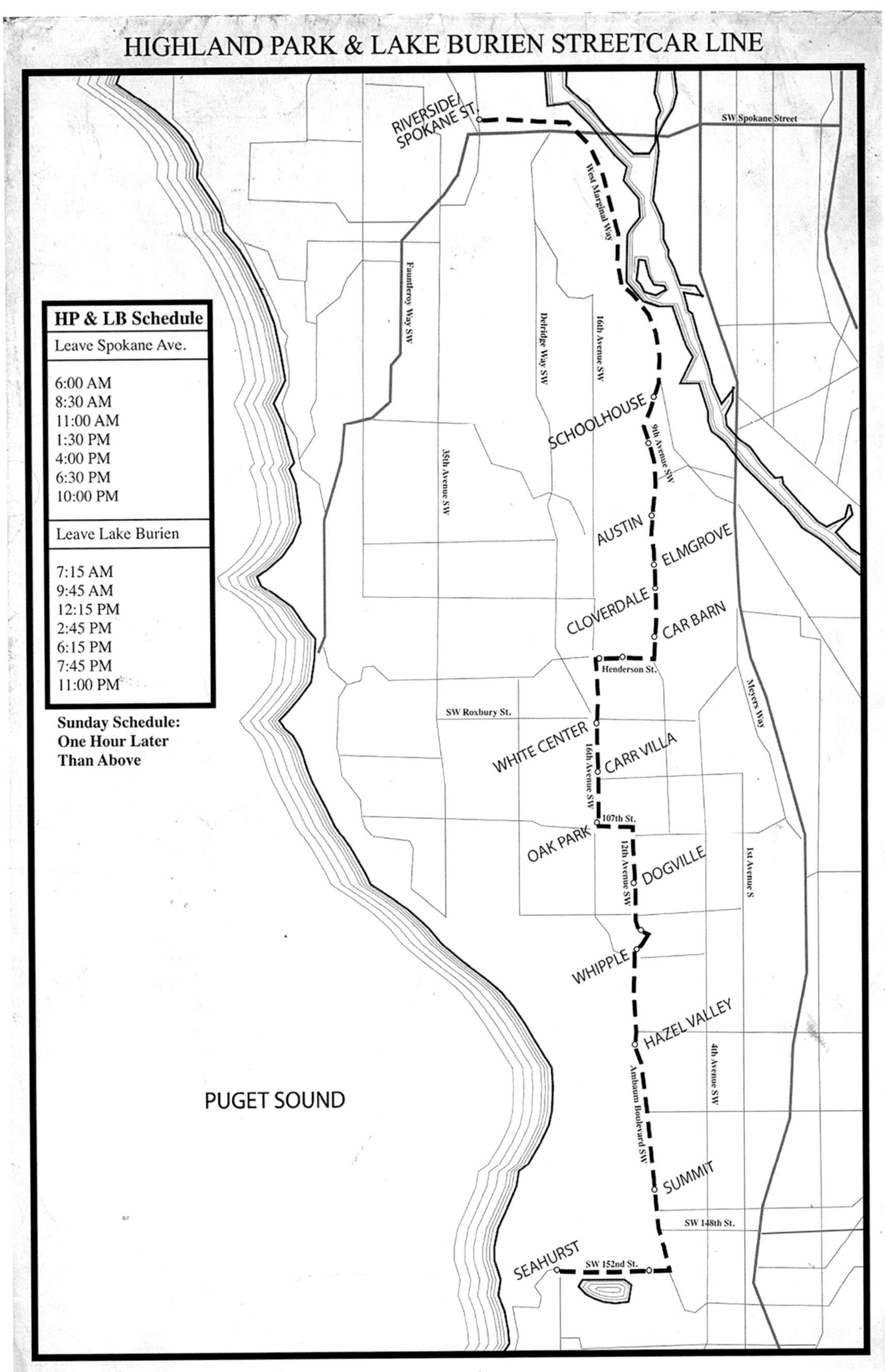

Map of Highland Park and Lake Burien line with 1912 schedule of departures.
Courtesy of Highline Heritage Museum.

a $2,500 bond. The number of jitneys on Seattle streets dropped significantly following passage of this legislation, but around 150 continued in operation.

The United States entered the war in Europe in April 1917, and the federal government quickly began a massive program to provide naval and merchant ships for the war effort. The Emergency Fleet Corporation (EFC), a government agency, was created to develop and oversee contracts for ship construction. Seattle's Elliott Bay shipyards, already busy, hummed with activity. Approximately 35,000 workers were employed in the yards and in associated trades by mid-1917. But the nearest streetcar lines were on First Avenue, and workers had to walk across a maze of active railroad tracks along the waterfront to reach their jobs. The influx of new residents also resulted in crush loads on the streetcars. PSTL&P was in a difficult position, since adding more streetcars and trainmen was an expensive commitment, and company officials were concerned that the ridership surge might be temporary. But the overcrowding resulted in considerable bad press for the company, and it was cited by municipal ownership advocates as another reason for the city to acquire all of the streetcar lines in Seattle.

PSTL&P also faced challenges on the labor front. By mid-1917, Local 587 of the Amalgamated Association of Street and Electric Railway Employees had organized nearly 100 percent of the company's operating staff. The union sought increased wages, an eight-hour day, and better working conditions. Workers went on strike in July 1917 after Leonard refused to negotiate. The company brought in hundreds of strikebreakers and attempted to resume service, but the climax was a violent struggle between strikebreakers, police, and union members at First Avenue and Yesler Way that resulted in twenty injured, two streetcars demolished, and several arrests. The strike occurred when World War I shipbuilding was at its height in Seattle, so Governor Ernest Lister stepped in to bring both sides together for talks. In a meeting with the governor, Leonard finally agreed to recognize the union and abide by the decision of an arbitration panel. The strike was over by August 2.[7]

Relations between PSTL&P and Seattle City Light grew increasingly hostile during this period. The private company had received a permit to develop a hydroelectric dam on the upper Skagit River in 1913 but had taken no action, and the permit was coming up for renewal. Following

Shipyard workers boarding crowded streetcars on First Avenue South near Massachusetts Street at shift change time, 1918. *PNRA photo WWASMR-DWNTN-008.*

protracted interactions with regulatory agencies, members of Congress, and the city council, Seattle City Light was authorized to construct the dam in late 1918. The episode caused great resentment at the private company, which believed it had first right of refusal for the Skagit site based on its initial permit application. Eventually the Skagit Project was to become the largest single source of electric power for Seattle City Light, and both utilities would compete for power customers in Seattle until Seattle City Light finally purchased PSTL&P's Seattle facilities in 1951.

At the Bargaining Table

Seattle's streetcar troubles came to a head in mid-1918. The Puget Sound Traction, Light and Power Company requested permission to raise fares following the strike but offered no assurances of increased service. The city of Seattle accused the company of not meeting its franchise obligations and ignoring its agreement to share the cost of new bridges. The Emergency Fleet Corporation brought pressure on the city, saying that unless it dealt successfully with the streetcar situation, the government would issue no more shipbuilding contracts to Seattle firms.

On September 6, 1918, PST&P president Leonard met with Mayor Ole Hanson, members of the city council, and Emergency Fleet Corporation representative A. Merritt Taylor. The meeting was held on the "neutral ground" of the New Washington Hotel in downtown Seattle. Leonard offered to sell the company's Seattle streetcar properties for $16 million, based on the total amount appraisers estimated had been invested in the system since 1899. Hanson quickly responded with a counteroffer of $15 million, supposedly based on a mile-for-mile comparison of what Division A had cost to build plus depreciation. Leonard immediately accepted. There was no discussion at the meeting of what exactly would and would not be included in the purchase, and no evidence that an inventory of the company's properties, equipment, and other assets had been provided. The city could not provide money up front but would purchase the system by issuing bonds to be paid from future streetcar fare revenue. The bonds would carry a 5 percent interest rate at a time when most municipal bonds were paying about 2.5 percent. The city was expected to pay about $833,000 annually in principal and interest for twenty years.

Seattle Mayor Ole Hanson. *Courtesy of the Seattle Municipal Archives, item 12281.*

The city council was bitterly divided but also weary of continuing to battle with PSTL&P and the Emergency Fleet Corporation. In a 5–4 vote, the council approved the purchase but made it conditioned on the result of an advisory ballot to be put before the voters on November 5, 1918. The city's three daily newspapers all supported the purchase, some even stating that the price was a bargain. In the midst of the worldwide flu epidemic, Seattle voters went to the polls and approved the purchase by a wide margin, with 13,000 in favor and only 4,000 opposed.

Most Seattle historians agree that the city paid an inflated price for the PSTL&P streetcar properties. The 1918 tax assessment of the properties valued them at only $5.6 million.[8] An investigation of the purchase conducted by a city legal team in late 1920 showed that the value of the properties did not exceed $7.8 million.[9] The official company history of the Puget Sound Power and Light Company (as PSTL&P was later renamed) suggests that Hanson was naïve about the street railway's finances:

> The public became convinced that by eliminating "those profiteers" (a wartime term of disapproval) the nickel streetcar fare could be preserved. Leonard knew better, but decided the best course was to sell out. Based on an independent appraisal value of $16 million, he negotiated with Mayor Ole Hanson a sale at $15 million, to be paid in the form of an issue of revenue bonds. When the city fathers later learned that, indeed, the system could not be profitable on the nickel fare, Leonard was accused of seducing Ole Hanson into paying too much for the system.[10]

What led Hanson and other elected officials to agree to such a deal? How realistic was it to expect fare revenue to pay for bond principal and interest, day-to-day operations, and capital investments in new streetcars and related infrastructure as the system wore out? Not realistic at all, it turned out. Perhaps they felt that, as a city department, the Municipal Railway would benefit from cost sharing with other utilities. Maybe the engineering department could pick up some streetcar-related costs, such as paving between the tracks and the street railway share of new bridge costs. Perhaps the streetcar electrical substations eventually could be turned over to Seattle

City Light with its lower power rates. At the time, all of this seemed to be within the realm of possibility, as city-owned streetcar systems were practically unknown elsewhere in the United States.

STREETCAR RAPID TRANSIT

To address the immediate shipyard transportation problem, Mayor Hanson put forward a plan to build an elevated streetcar trestle between Pioneer Square and Spokane Street. The trestle would start at First Avenue and Washington Street, serve the shipyards directly along the Elliott Bay waterfront, and continue south along Railroad Avenue (now Alaskan Way) and East Marginal Way to Spokane Street. At this point it would join another streetcar trestle already under construction that crossed Harbor Island and ended at a swing span bridge crossing the West Waterway of the Duwamish River. The tracks

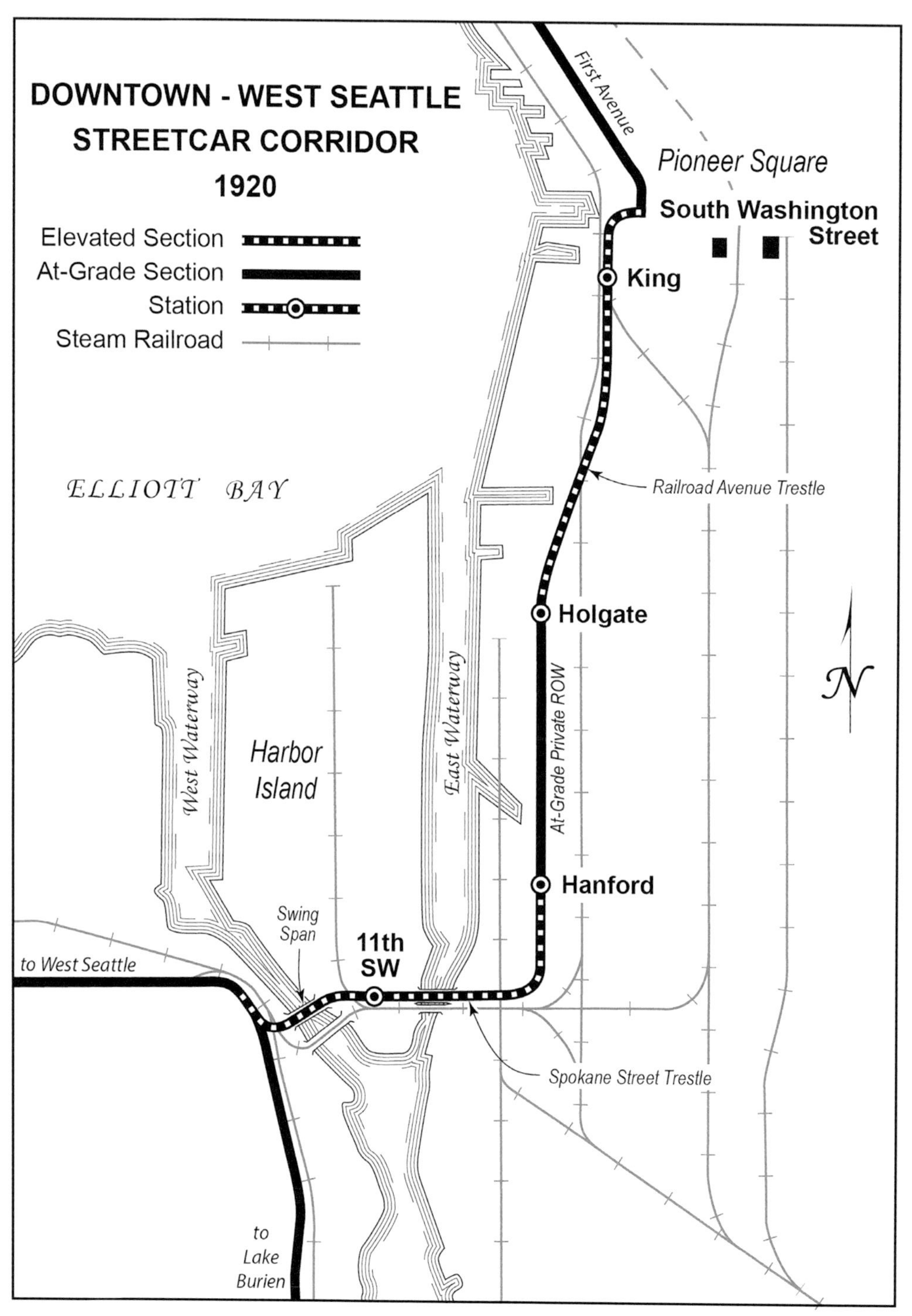

Downtown–West Seattle streetcar corridor showing elevated and surface sections, 1920. *Map by Dave Cooley.*

would then drop down to the surface on the west side of the bridge and continue to West Seattle and Burien. Four intermediate passenger stations would be provided on the streetcar trestle, at King Street, Holgate Street, Hanford Street, and Harbor Island. The elevated trestle would increase the speed, reliability, and capacity of the four streetcar routes serving West Seattle, effectively providing a lengthy section of rail rapid transit. A $350,000 bond issue to construct the Railroad Avenue elevated was included as a separate measure on the November 5, 1918, ballot and was approved by voters. Construction started in January 1919, and the double-track elevated trestle was completed and opened for service just nine months later.

While the Railroad Avenue elevated clearly improved the quality of service for West Seattle riders, its original purpose—facilitating transportation to the shipyards—quickly became less crucial. The war ended on November 11, 1918, and it didn't take long for the Emergency Fleet Corporation to cancel most of the ship building contracts. Nevertheless, total system ridership continued to set records: 133 million passengers in 1919, an all-time high for streetcars in Seattle.

Harbor Island Station on Spokane Street trestle with streetcar at platform, 1919. *PNRA photo WWASMR-SPO-044.*

Seattle Streetcar Routes, January 1, 1918

Routes operated by the Puget Sound Traction, Light and Power Company and predecessors:

Yesler Way Cable: Initial segment opened in 1888 by the Seattle Construction Company.

Madison Street Cable: Initial segment opened in 1890 by the Madison Street Cable Railway Company.

James Street Cable: Opened in 1891 by the Union Trunk Line.

Route 1, Alki Point: Opened in 1907 by the Seattle Electric Company.

Route 2, Fauntleroy Park: Opened in 1907 by the Seattle Electric Company.

Route 4, West Seattle Ferry Dock–West Seattle Junction: Opened in 1902 by the West Seattle Municipal Railway.

Route 5, South Park: Opened in 1892 by the Grant Street Electric Railway via Georgetown; rerouted via First Avenue South in 1909 by the Seattle Electric Company.

Route 6, South Seattle: Opened in 1892 by the Grant Street Electric Railway; originally combined with South Park route. Truncated at Carleton Avenue South and East Marginal Way South (Georgetown) by the Seattle Electric Company when South Park service rerouted via First Avenue South in 1909.

Route 7, Kinnear Park: Initial segment opened in 1892 by the Seattle Consolidated Railway Company.

Route 8, East Union–Downtown–Twenty-Sixth Avenue South: East Union segment opened in 1903, Twenty-Sixth Avenue South segment opened in 1908, both by the Seattle Electric Company.

Route 9, Nineteenth Avenue–Downtown–Mount Baker Park: Nineteenth Avenue segment opened in 1907, Mount Baker segment opened 1908, both by the Seattle Electric Company.

Route 10, Twenty-Third Avenue: Opened in 1909 by the Seattle Electric Company.

Route 11, Madrona Park: Initial segment opened in 1892 by the Union Trunk Line.

Route 12, East Madison–Downtown–Beacon Hill: East Madison segment opened in 1910 by the Seattle Electric Company, replacing 1890 cable line east of Fourteenth Avenue. The initial Beacon Hill segment was opened in 1891 by the Union Trunk Line.

Route 13, Summit: Opened in 1907 by the Seattle Electric Company.

Route 14, Capitol Hill: Opened in 1903 by the Seattle Central Railway Company.

Route 15, Broadway: Initial segment opened by the Union Trunk Line in 1892.

Route 16, Ravenna Park: Opened in 1891 by the Rainier Power and Railway Company.

Route 17, North Fortieth Street: Opened in 1910 by the Seattle Electric Company as a branch of Route 16; converted to shuttle in 1915.

Route 18, Wallingford: Opened 1907 by the Seattle Electric Company.

Route 19, West Woodland/Sixth Avenue NW: Opened in 1911 by the Seattle Electric Company.

Route 20, Green Lake: Initial segment opened in 1890 by the Green Lake Electric Railway Company.

Route 21, Phinney: Initial segment opened in 1890 by the Woodland Park Electric Railway Company.

Route 22, Meridian: Opened 1907 by Seattle Electric Company.

Route 23, Fremont–Ballard: Initial segment opened in 1902 by the Seattle Electric Company.

Route 24, North Queen Anne: Initial segment opened in 1892 by the Seattle Consolidated Railway Company.

Route 25, East Queen Anne: Initial segment opened in 1892 by the Seattle Consolidated Railway Company.

Route 26, West Queen Anne: Initial segment opened by the Front Street Cable Railway Company in 1891 as a cable line between Pioneer Square and Highland Drive on Queen Anne Hill. Converted to an electric car line by the Seattle Electric Company in 1901 with a counterbalance system assisting the cars on Queen Anne Hill.

Route 27, Ballard North: Initial segment opened in 1891 by the West Street and North End Electric Railway Company.

Route 28, Ballard Beach: Opened in 1906 by Seattle Electric Company between Ballard Beach and downtown Ballard, then via Route 27 track to downtown Seattle. Later redesignated Route 30, Sunset Hill.

Route 29, Fort Lawton: Opened in 1905 by the Seattle Electric Company.

ROUTES OPERATED BY THE SEATTLE MUNICIPAL STREET RAILWAY AND PREDECESSORS:

Division A: Initial segment between Loyal Heights and Ballard opened in 1906 by the Loyal Railway. Merged in 1918 with Seattle Municipal Street Railway Division A, which opened between downtown and the Ballard Bridge in 1914 via Dexter Avenue and Nickerson Street.

Division C: Opened in 1912 by the Highland Park and Lake Burien Railroad between Lake Burien and Riverside (Spokane and Twenty-Third Avenue SW). Donated to the city of Seattle in 1913.

ROUTES OPERATED BY SEATTLE AND RAINIER VALLEY RAILWAY AND PREDECESSORS:

Main Line: Initial segment opened in 1891 by the Rainier Avenue Electric Railway between downtown Seattle and Columbia City; extended to Renton in 1896. The final corporate name was the Seattle and Rainier Valley Railway Company, adopted in 1916.

Genesee Shuttle: Opened in 1917 by the Seattle and Rainier Valley Railway Company.

A CITYWIDE MUNICIPAL RAILWAY

On April 1, 1919, the city of Seattle took possession of the former Puget Sound Traction, Light and Power Company streetcar properties, which consisted of 194 miles of electric railway track, 8.6 miles of cable car track, 477 passenger cars, 27 freight motor cars, and 36 nonmotorized freight and work cars. The purchase also included the overhead trolley and feeder distribution system, four electric car barns, three cable car barns, and the large car repair shop in Georgetown. The company's route numbering system was retained with some modifications: Division A became Route 6 and Division C became Route 4. The cable car and neighborhood shuttle lines remained unnumbered. (See list of all Seattle streetcar routes prior to Seattle Municipal Street Railway–PSTL&P consolidation.)

PSTL&P retained ownership of the streetcar power substations, but the "Traction" part of the company's name was dropped following the sale of the Seattle streetcar properties. Thereafter, the official corporate title became Puget Sound Power and Light Company. (The company is referred to as "Puget Power" from this point on in the book.) At the city of Seattle, the Division of Street Railways established its administrative office in Room 507 of the County-City Building. The name appearing on correspondence, on transfer slips, and on the sides of the streetcar barns now read "Seattle

Municipal Street Railway," although it was commonly shortened to just "Municipal Railway."

The first year of the consolidated system was tumultuous. Many Puget Power streetcar employees took advantage of an opportunity to stay with the private company in another job position, forcing the city to quickly recruit and train replacements. The company had also deferred track maintenance on some routes due to wartime conditions. These circumstances, together with what can best be described as a "perfect storm" of errors and miscalculations, led to a string of serious streetcar accidents through the remainder of 1919 and the first part of 1920. On one particularly bad day, October 28, 1919, a Phinney car derailed making the turn from North Forty-Third Street to Fremont Avenue and turned on its side; a Kinnear car derailed at Second Avenue West and Roy Street and hit a telephone pole; and a West Queen Anne car went out of control on the counterbalance, left the rails, and was finally stopped by a high curb. All of these accidents resulted in injuries. The most serious accident during this period occurred on January 5, 1920, when a Green Lake streetcar went out of control heading downhill on Woodland Park Avenue at North Thirty-Eighth Street. The car struck a telephone pole and was virtually cut in half. One passenger was killed and seventy-five were injured, many seriously.[11]

These accidents made headlines in the city's four daily newspapers, and citizens looked for someone to blame. In light of the city's recent purchase of the privately owned system, many suspected under-the-table bribery, gross incompetence on the part of municipal management, or some combination of both. While there were many divergent views on what the causes were, the notion of municipal ownership as a cure-all for the streetcar system quickly fell out of favor.

Wreck of car #721 at Woodland Park Avenue and North Thirty-Eighth Street on Green Lake line, January 1920. *PNRA photo WWAST-20-027.*

The 1920s:
Bought but Not Paid For

Against this background of accidents and operator shortages, the Seattle Municipal Railway made some genuine progress during its first year of consolidated operation. The Division A carbarn on Third Avenue West was sold and the line's complex double trolley wire overhead was replaced with the single-wire system used throughout the rest of the city. Transfers were now issued and accepted on all lines. Double track on Avalon Way and Fauntleroy Avenue replaced the original steep and circuitous single track between Spokane Street and the West Seattle Junction. Significantly, the Municipal Railway continued the private company's program of converting streetcar lines from two-man to one-man operation to reduce operating costs, although initial progress was slow because of the safety modifications needed on the cars and an agreement with the union that the conversion would not result in employee layoffs.

The First Buses

Perhaps the most overlooked milestone during this first year was the start-up of the Municipal Railway's first bus line. From the beginning, proponents of municipal ownership argued that only a publicly owned system would be motivated to provide comprehensive, citywide service. Little funding was available to extend streetcar lines into developing neighborhoods, but bus service required a

Municipal Railway Ford bus #101 on Carleton Park route shortly after service started, 1919. *PNRA photo WWASMR-BUS-101-001.*

relatively modest up-front investment. Magnolia had been part of Seattle since 1891, but only the northern end of the bluff (Route 29 to Fort Lawton) was served by streetcars. By the late 1910s and early 1920s, real estate developers were subdividing the central and southern parts of the bluff, and the population was steadily increasing. To meet the area's transportation needs, the railway established a short bus line connecting Carleton Park with existing streetcar lines at Fifteenth Avenue West and West Dravus Street. The service began operation on November 28, 1919.

The new Magnolia service established a blueprint for most of the later bus lines operated by the Municipal Railway. Railway managers initially viewed buses as a low-capacity form of public transportation, to be used as an interim step to build ridership in developing areas until streetcar extensions could be funded and built. Buses were most suitable on short neighborhood shuttle routes with light passenger loads, making connections with streetcar routes rather than offering through service to downtown. Given the state of bus technology in 1919, it is not difficult to see the logic of this approach. Buses of the era were slow, hard riding and had limited seating and standing room. The buses used on the Carleton Park route were based on a Ford Model T truck chassis and had home-built wooden bodies with seats for just sixteen passengers. Based on customer complaints, it appears that the bodies were not well sealed and engine exhaust often seeped into the passenger compartment. But the capital cost of the buses was relatively low, and they obviously did not require tracks and overhead wires, so service could be implemented quickly and routes could easily be changed as ridership and other factors dictated. The Municipal Railway eventually set aside space in the North Seattle, Fremont, and Massachusetts Street carbarns to provide storage and maintenance facilities for the bus fleet.

A second bus route quickly followed the Carleton Park start-up. On April 1, 1920, the Municipal Railway began service on Thirty-Fifth Avenue SW in West Seattle, operating from the streetcar stop at Thirty-Fifth and Avalon to Thirty-Fifth and Roxbury Street. Municipal Railway officials felt that this corridor eventually would be able to support streetcar service, and maps and other documents indicate that this was the intent well into the 1930s.

Throughout the 1920s the Municipal Railway continued to expand bus service into developing neighborhoods that the streetcars did not reach. New bus routes were started serving Admiral Way, Delridge Way, Empire Way (now Martin Luther King Jr. Way), Roosevelt Way, and Laurelhurst. All of these services were feeder lines that connected with streetcar routes. In April 1925, buses replaced streetcars for the first time when the North Fortieth Street shuttle was converted to rubber-tired vehicles. This short route, originally a branch of the Eastlake line, made connections with downtown streetcars

Municipal Railway White bus #134 at terminal of Empire Way route, 1926. *PNRA photo WWASMR-BUS-134-001.*

at the University Bridge and at Wallingford Avenue and North Fortieth Street.

FREIGHT SERVICE

In an era before the widespread use of trucks, street railways provided a way to ship and receive carloads of freight directly to the doors of local businesses not served by steam railroads. Freight cars were moved by small electric locomotives or by "box motors," electric cars that looked like conventional streetcars with covered-over windows. The Municipal Railway had operated freight service on Division C (the former Highland Park and Lake Burien line) since 1914, and it inherited Puget Power's freight operation with the 1919 consolidation. Local businesses served included lumberyards, brickworks, canneries, coal dealers, and storage warehouses. Division C even had a spur that served the original Boeing Airplane Company on West Marginal Way. The Seattle Municipal Railway interchanged with the Great Northern Railway at Ballard, with the Northern Pacific Railway at Fremont and Youngstown, and with both railroads plus the Union Pacific at Georgetown. Freight operations generally were carried out late at night to avoid conflicts with passenger service. The Municipal Railway had its own fleet of freight cars, but they were used primarily for delivering track, paving materials, and overhead trolley wire to streetcar lines undergoing repair and maintenance. Most cars used in revenue freight service were owned by the steam railroads.

With improvements to truck technology and the widespread expansion of paved streets, the Municipal Railway's freight operations declined rapidly during the 1920s, and all freight service was gone by 1930.

A LEGAL RULING WITH DIRE CONSEQUENCES

Former city attorney Hugh Caldwell ran for mayor in early 1920 on a platform that included investigating the Municipal Railway purchase. He easily won in the March 3 election and made good on his promise by initiating a comprehensive review of the Puget Power deal and a thorough appraisal of the company's streetcar properties. While these efforts uncovered few facts that weren't already known, they did confirm the inflated purchase price the city agreed to and the role that the Emergency Fleet Corporation had played in pressuring the city to take over the system. The new mayor followed up by firing the first superintendent of the consolidated municipal system, Thomas Murphine, a close friend of former mayor Ole Hanson. Most important, the long-established nickel fare was raised to 10 cents cash, or four tokens for 25 cents, effective June 1, 1920. The large increase was explained as necessary to put the system on a sound financial basis, but the cumulative public resentment over this and other events related to

Box motor pulling freight train on west side of Green Lake, circa 1920. *PNRA photo WWASMR-020-024.*

the Puget Power deal lasted for years afterward.

By December 1920 the Municipal Railway was still facing a large cash shortage from the previous nine months, much of it related to the start-up costs of consolidation, major accident claims, the need to recruit and train new operating employees, and a general economic recession. The city transferred $83,000 from the general fund to the street railway fund to meet the employee payroll. The transaction was considered a loan, with the expectation that the Municipal Railway would reimburse the general fund for the same amount within a year, which it did.

In what became known as the *Asia v. City of Seattle* case, fourteen taxpayers immediately brought suit against the city to return the $83,000 to the general fund. It also sought to enjoin the city from using the general fund or levying any tax for the operation and maintenance of the Seattle Municipal Railway. The case eventually made its way to the state supreme court. On April 29, 1922, the court ruled in favor of the plaintiffs. Writing for the majority, Justice J. Tolman stated:

> We are not now concerned with questions other than the one before us, and are not called upon to advise the city how, if at all, it may solve the serious problem which has arisen from what has proven to be the erroneous judgment of its legislative body, but we are clear that only one construction can be placed upon the statute which governs this situation, and that is that when it is proposed that any general indebtedness be incurred for such a purpose as is here considered, the matter must be submitted to the voters, and if not so submitted all obligations arising from the acquisition, operation and maintenance of the utility must be met from its revenue, and in any event, by no action of the city or its officials can the burden be shifted to the shoulders of the taxpayers, who have had no opportunity to say whether they will or will not accept the hazard.[1]

The city was thus prohibited from using taxpayer-provided funds to support the Municipal Railway unless the funds were specifically approved by the voters for such purposes. The court did clarify that short-term loans from other city departments were allowable. But given the public's opinion of the Municipal Railway in 1922, city officials were understandably reluctant to even consider putting a "Save Our Streetcars" proposition on the ballot.

In the months before the supreme court ruling, the financial situation of the Municipal Railway was becoming increasingly precarious. To meet the first bond payment, the railway had to come up with $833,000 by September 1, 1921. To meet the deadline and avoid default, it withheld paychecks from its employees during July, issuing them promissory notes (called warrants) instead. This happened twice again during 1922. Gradually the improving economy resulted in increased ridership, and—together with operating efficiencies and another fare increase—the system was able to provide full back pay to its employees plus interest.

A major cost-cutting effort was initiated. Between 1921 and 1924, twelve streetcar lines were converted from two-man to one-man operation. On May 21, 1921, the West Seattle carbarn was closed and the West Seattle routes were shifted to the North Seattle carbarn. On April 2, 1923, all regular passenger service was discontinued on the Western Avenue line. Various route hookups were implemented to reduce duplicative car miles through the central business district. For example, the Capitol Hill and Mount Baker lines, instead of operating separately and overlapping each other through downtown, were combined as one route starting in March 1922. Some of these route combinations became permanent, while others were later broken up due to load imbalance or on-time performance issues.

Streetcar Extensions and Abandonments

Two significant extensions were added to the Municipal Railway streetcar network during the 1920s. By the end of 1924 the financial crisis had eased to the point where the railway established a small renewal and betterment fund. Also, the state supreme court decision did not prohibit outside parties from providing assistance to the Municipal Railway.

In northeastern Seattle, the Maple Leaf neighborhood was filling in with new homes, but the nearest streetcar service was the Ravenna line at Fifteenth Avenue NE and Cowen Place, more than a mile south of the city limits at Eighty-Fifth Street. The Municipal Railway's correspondence files suggest that neighborhood developers agreed to pay for certain costs related to an extension to Maple Leaf, including paving between the tracks. The city constructed a temporary timber bridge across the Ravenna Park ravine, and track was built north on Fifteenth Avenue NE from the bridge to a new turnaround at NE Eightieth Street just south of the Bothell Highway (now Lake City Way). Streetcars serving the new extension were designated Route 17, and service began on December 1, 1925.

More ambitious was the extension of Route 10–Montlake. This line originally ended at the south gate of the 1909 Alaska-Yukon-Pacific Exposition, which occupied the University of Washington campus. As

Route 17/Fifteenth Avenue NE streetcar #268 at NE Eightieth Street terminal wye, 1940. *PNRA photo WWASMR-017-012.*

Route 10/Montlake streetcar #387 operating westbound by the University of Washington golf course (now UW Medical Center), 1940. NE Pacific Street is on the right. *PNRA photo WWASMR-010-001.*

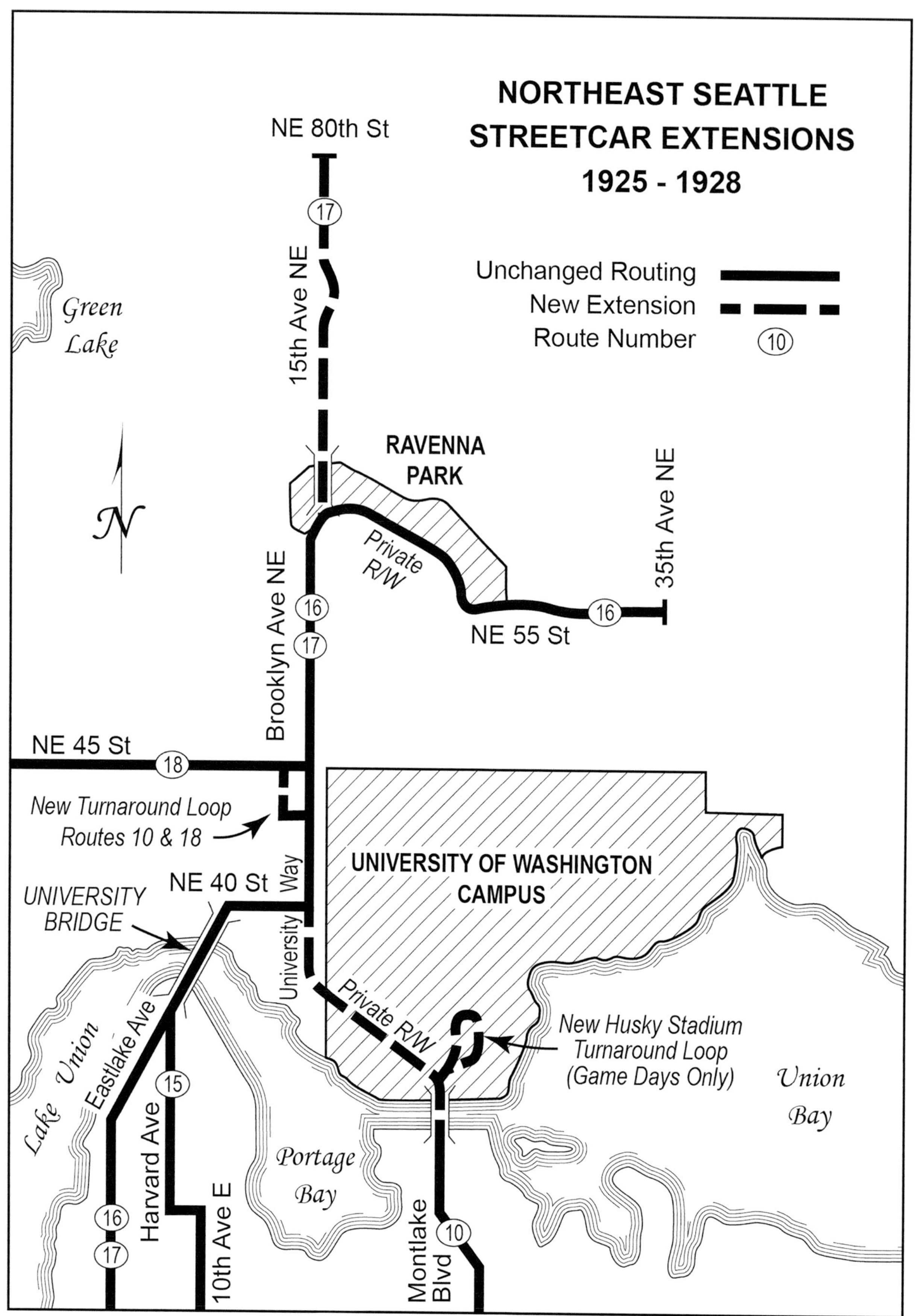

Northeast Seattle Route Changes, 1925–1928. *Map by Dave Cooley.*

part of the Lake Washington Ship Canal project, the Montlake canal was completed between Portage Bay and Union Bay in 1917. This truncated the streetcar line just south of the canal, isolating it from the university. A temporary bridge carried motor vehicle traffic across the canal, but it had no streetcar tracks. The city, using both state and federal funds, constructed a permanent Montlake bridge that included tracks and opened it on July 27, 1925. At about the same time, the University of Washington funded construction of a streetcar loop and passenger loading platform for Husky Stadium on the north side of the new bridge. The university also provided right-of-way for a streetcar extension along the south side of Pacific Street, now the site of University of Washington Medical Center. New track was laid on this right-of-way and extended north on University Way to NE Fortieth Street, where it connected with the existing Broadway and Ravenna Park lines. The 0.8-mile Montlake extension was completed and opened for service on May 16, 1928. The new track layout allowed streetcars from the Broadway and Ravenna Park lines to serve Husky Stadium during major events, in addition to the Montlake route. (See map "Northeast Seattle Route Changes, 1925–1928.")

Some vestiges of the overbuilt streetcar network from the 1890s and early 1900s persisted into the early Municipal Railway era. When the new double-track alignment between Spokane Street and West Seattle Junction opened in 1919, the railway continued to operate a shuttle streetcar on a segment of the old track that served the Youngstown business district on SW Andover Street. It was abandoned on December 3, 1928. Also abandoned in 1928 was the Ray Street Shuttle, a 1,300-foot-long streetcar line that operated on Queen Anne Avenue between Ray Street and Boston Street (the spelling of "Ray" Street was later changed to "Raye" Street). During off-peak periods, there was no set schedule, and passengers pushed a button at their stop to signal the motorman to come pick them up. In Ballard, a local shuttle streetcar operated on Twentieth Avenue NW from Ballard Avenue to NW Sixty-Seventh Street. It survived until January 1, 1931.

Ballard Route Changes

One route connecting Ballard with downtown Seattle underwent major restructuring during the 1920s. The Ballard North streetcar line started at Fourteenth Avenue NW and NW Seventieth Street and operated south on Fourteenth to Ballard Way, which accounts for the wide center median that exists on Fourteenth today. From Ballard Way, the route continued to downtown Seattle using the Fremont Bridge and Westlake Avenue.

Streetcar #737 operating southbound on Fifteenth Avenue NW near NE Eightieth Street, 1939. *PNRA photo WWASMR-027-027.*

In 1905, track was laid on Fifteenth Avenue NW in Ballard for the first segment of the Seattle–Everett Interurban, but after Stone & Webster acquired the interurban company the Everett service switched to the more direct Phinney Avenue line as its entry into downtown Seattle. This left the Fifteenth Avenue NW track as part of a lightly used shuttle line between Ballard and Greenwood. In 1918 the city opened the current Ballard Bridge on the Fifteenth Avenue alignment, and the Ballard Beach and Ballard–Loyal Heights streetcar routes began using it to reach downtown. During 1926, the Municipal Railway rebuilt the Fifteenth Avenue NW track and shifted the Ballard North streetcar line to it on July 27, 1927. In addition to a more direct route to downtown using the new Ballard Bridge and Elliott Avenue, this change allowed service to be extended from Seventieth Street to Eighty-Fifth Street, then the northern city limits. The Fourteenth Avenue trackage was abandoned shortly after the changeover, and the new route was renamed Fifteenth Avenue NW. (See map of Northwest Seattle route changes.)

West Seattle Bridges

While West Seattle streetcars used the congestion-free elevated trestle route between downtown and Harbor Island, they shared right-of-way with other vehicles on the Spokane Street swing span over the Duwamish River's West Waterway. This bridge, completed in 1917, was a temporary wooden structure with a roadway only twenty feet wide, barely enough for two streetcars to pass and hazardous for large motor vehicles. Streetcars left the bridge at each end by separate wooden trestle approaches.

While the city's intent was to replace the swing span with two permanent bascule bridges built of steel and concrete, final approval and funding for Bridge No. 1 was not secured until March 1923. The new bridge was constructed north of the old one, and while it was

Old Spokane Street wooden swing span bridge with new Bridge No. 1 completed to the north, 1925. *PNRA photo WWASMR-SPO-021.*

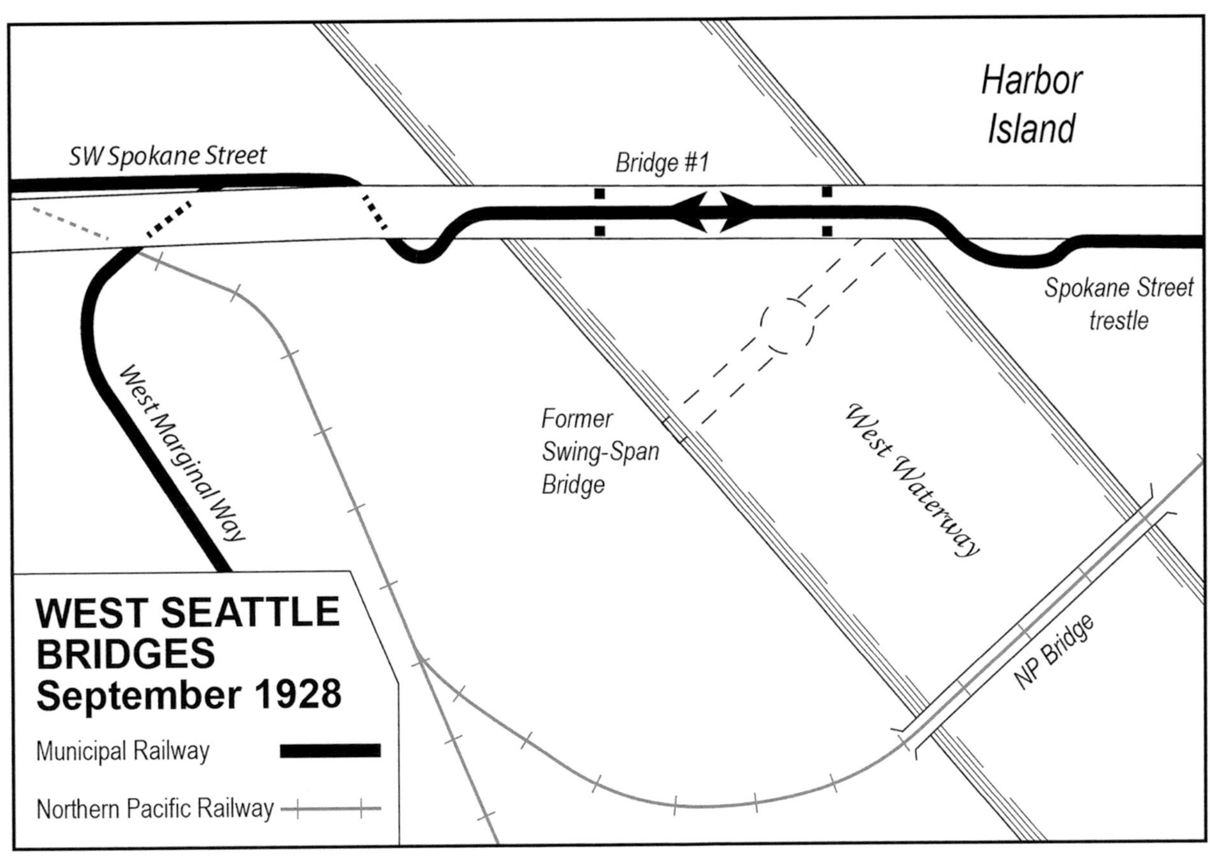

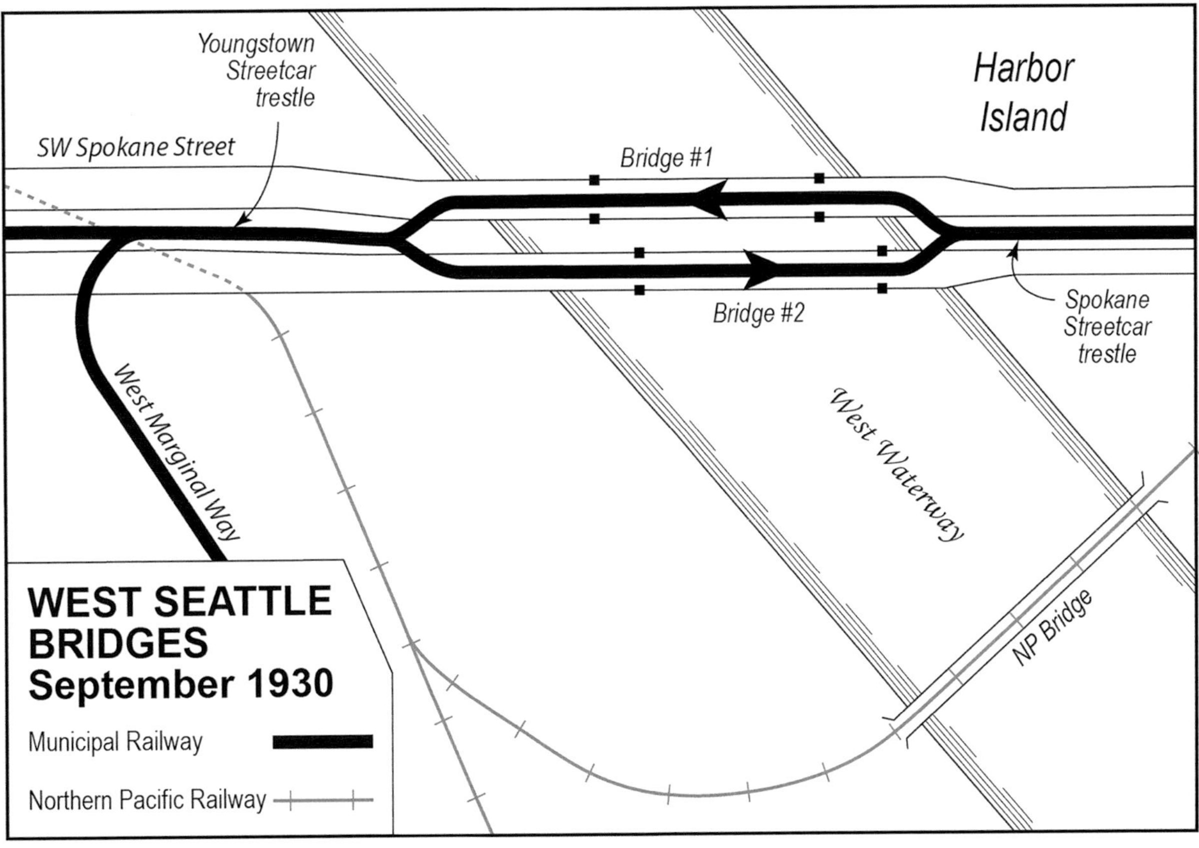

Spokane Street bridge changes between 1928 and 1930. *Map by Dave Cooley.*

Westbound streetcar entering Bridge No. 1 in heavy auto traffic, May 1930. *PNRA photo WWASMR-SPO-034.*

Streetcar #278 eastbound on Youngstown streetcar trestle with elevated station at Twenty-Third Avenue SW and SW Spokane Street in background, 1940. *PNRA photo WWASMR-SPO-014.*

Streetcar descending from Railroad Avenue elevated to First and Washington, looking south, July 20, 1929. *PNRA photo WWASMR-SPO-066.*

Hanford Street Station on Railroad Avenue streetcar line looking north, late 1920s. *PNRA photo WWASMR-SPO-059.*

Severed end of Railroad Avenue trestle looking northeast from Spokane Street following abandonment, October 1929. *PNRA photo WWASMR-SPO-058.*

strong enough to carry streetcars, no rails were laid on the bridge deck. After completion of Bridge No. 1 in December 1924, the old wooden swing span was used exclusively by streetcars. In late 1927, test borings revealed serious weaknesses in the central foundation piling of the swing span. On January 13, 1928, it was closed to streetcar traffic, and passengers were forced to walk across the bridge and transfer to waiting streetcars on either side. On January 15, work started to modify the track connections so that streetcars could use Bridge No. 1. By performing as much work as possible in advance of this date, the connections were complete by January 21, allowing through service to be restored.

The new access to Bridge No. 1 required streetcars to make unprotected turns from the approach trestles to the traffic lanes on the bridge. By 1928, motor vehicle volume to and from West Seattle was heavy, and streetcars were often delayed waiting for gaps in the traffic. This shortcoming was addressed in the design of Bridge No. 2, which was built south of No. 1 on the site of the old swing span. With the completion of No. 2 in September 1930, westbound streetcars used the inside traffic lane on Bridge No. 1 and eastbound cars used the inside lane on Bridge No. 2, thus minimizing conflicts between streetcars and other traffic. Making this change possible was construction of a new concrete streetcar viaduct through Youngstown, which included a redesigned approach to the two newer bridges. The Youngstown viaduct also featured an elevated passenger station at Twenty-Third Avenue SW and Spokane Street, where connections were made between streetcars and feeder buses.[2]

A Lost Opportunity: The Railroad Avenue Elevated

The Seattle Municipal Railway's financial difficulties led to deferred maintenance in a number of areas, including the Railroad Avenue elevated streetcar trestle, which carried West Seattle streetcars between Pioneer Square and Spokane Street. Completed in just nine months during 1919, the structure was constructed of timber "bents" similar to mainline railroad trestles and had three intermediate passenger stations with wooden platforms. It actually was two trestles, the northern one running from Washington Street to Holgate Street, followed by a short section of surface operation, then ramping up again at Hanford Street before reaching the Spokane Street trestle.

Periodically inspected by the city's bridge engineer, the northern segment of the Railroad Avenue trestle showed signs of serious deterioration and was condemned on October 12, 1929, ten years after it opened. As a structure used exclusively by Municipal Railway streetcars, there was simply no funding to repair or replace it. Over the next two

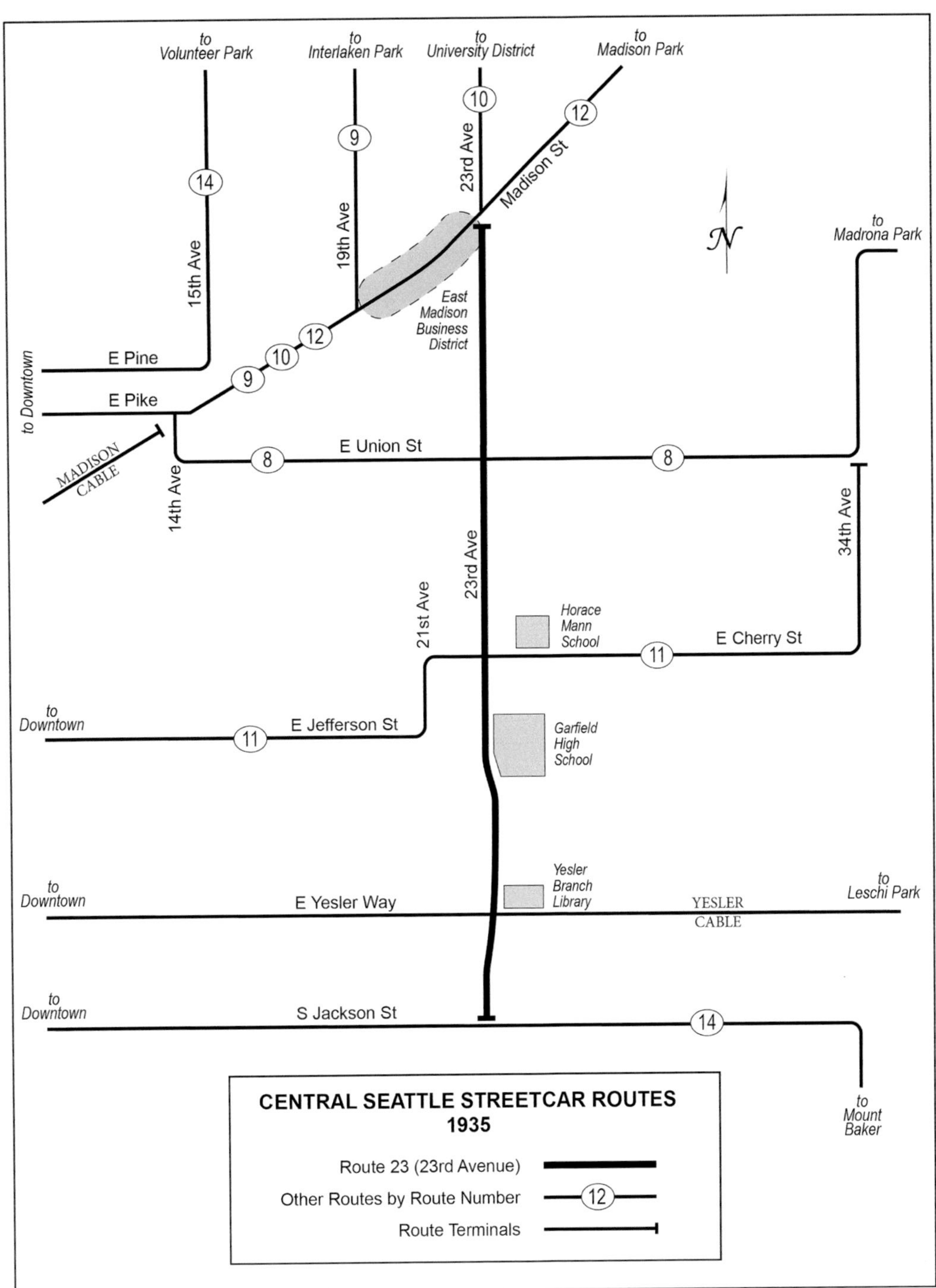

Central Seattle streetcar routes with Route 23 highlighted. *Map by Dave Cooley.*

days the connection between the Railroad Avenue trestle and the Spokane Street trestle was severed. A new streetcar ramp was built from First Avenue South to connect with the Spokane Street trestle, and buses shuttled streetcar passengers between Youngstown and First Avenue South during the changeover. On October 14, through streetcar service between West Seattle and downtown resumed using existing Route 5–South Park track on First Avenue South, a street that carried heavy automobile traffic.

While partially offset by the opening of West Spokane Street Bridge No. 2 and the short Youngstown viaduct the following year, the loss of the Railroad Avenue streetcar trestle eliminated a segment of what could accurately be called "rapid transit"—a high-volume transit route that was fully separated from other traffic. During the 1950s the trestle right-of-way was used to construct State Route 99, a limited-access roadway for motor vehicles.

Streetcars and Seattle's Black Neighborhoods

African Americans in Seattle represented about 1 percent of the city's total population during most of the streetcar era. In 1940 there were 3,789 Black residents in Seattle when the total city population was just over 368,000. While the Black population was comparatively small, it was concentrated heavily in just three central Seattle neighborhoods: near Twelfth Avenue and Jackson Street, Twenty-Third Avenue and Jackson Street, and Twenty-Third Avenue and East Madison Street. This highly segregated pattern resulted from discriminatory real estate practices such as redlining and deeds with racially restrictive covenants. However, all three areas had high levels of Municipal Railway streetcar service, which was vital in providing access to jobs, education, and shopping for basic necessities.

The Black community centered on East Madison Street has a particularly interesting history. William Grose, a Black Navy veteran, arrived in Seattle in 1858 and opened a hotel in Pioneer Square. He became friends with Henry Yesler, owner of a large sawmill and the town's major employer. In 1891, Grose acquired a large amount of property in the eastern Madison Hill area in settlement of a debt. That same year the Madison Cable Railway was completed between downtown Seattle and Madison Park, and the company's combination carbarn/powerhouse was erected on the south side of East Madison Street at Twenty-Second Avenue adjacent to the Grose properties. It was a large facility with boilers, two stationary steam engines, car maintenance and repair shops, and an enclosed car storage area. Many employees were needed to operate and maintain the complex. While no direct evidence has been uncovered, it is likely that residents of the neighborhood were employed at the carbarn.

With Grose as a major property owner, the area attracted Black families who were turned away from settling in other parts of the city. Black-owned businesses opened along Madison between Nineteenth and Twenty-Third Avenues, and Black churches established a long-term presence in the community. Strict lines of segregation existed at Thomas Street to the north and Twenty-Ninth Avenue to the east because of restrictive deed covenants. But compared with other Black neighborhoods in Seattle, the East Madison community was relatively stable and included merchants, postal employees, and railroad workers.[3]

By 1920 two additional streetcar lines served the area. The Madison carbarn/powerhouse was closed in 1910 when the cable line was truncated at Fourteenth Avenue, but service to East Madison was replaced by an electric line operating to downtown via East Pike Street. Route 10–Montlake provided service directly from East Madison to the University District, and the Route 23 streetcar provided crosstown service between Twenty-Third and Madison and Twenty-Third and Jackson, connecting two of the city's largest Black neighborhoods. In short, there was streetcar service in four directions from the intersection of Twenty-Third and Madison, providing many mobility options for neighborhood residents. (See map of Central Seattle streetcar routes.)

With the abandonment of all rail service in 1940–41, the Twenty-Third Avenue streetcar became a motor bus route, but only for a short time. By May 1944 even the bus route was gone, part of an effort by the Seattle Transit System to shift resources to more heavily used routes that served defense industries. The abandonment eliminated the direct connection between two Black neighborhoods along Twenty-Third Avenue; now a trip from East Madison to East Jackson Street required a transfer and a lengthy roundabout path through downtown Seattle. It would take over twenty years to restore a direct connection.

With the advent of the civil rights movement and the Model Cities Program in the 1960s, civic leaders pressed Seattle Transit to again provide a crosstown bus route through central Seattle. The result was Route 48, started in September 1966, which operated along Twenty-Third Avenue all the way from Rainier Avenue to the University District. It was the first new full-time Seattle bus route since World War II. Route 48 was successful, and today it is one of King County Metro's busiest routes.

Struggling Toward Stability

During the 1920s the use of private automobiles skyrocketed in Seattle, as elsewhere in the United States. By 1930, 90,000 cars were registered in Seattle. Mass production and standardized designs had brought the price of cars within reach of millions of families. Governments at all levels were rushing to build new roads and expand existing ones.

After reaching a peak of 133 million riders in 1919, Seattle streetcar ridership dropped precipitously, down to 92 million in 1925. But for the remainder of the decade the decline slowed. It was still above 89 million in 1929, the year of the stock market crash. Given the transportation revolution that was taking place and the financial problems besetting the Municipal Railway, it seems remarkable that ridership remained as stable as it did.

Mayor Bertha Landes. *Courtesy of the Seattle Municipal Archives, item 12285.*

Mayor Frank Edwards. *Courtesy of the Seattle Municipal Archives, item 12286.*

In late 1926 it appeared likely that the Municipal Railway would again be unable to make the annual payment on the purchase bond. Seattle mayor Bertha Landes asked Seattle City Light superintendent J. D. Ross for a loan to cover the railway's immediate payroll expenses, a request that he reluctantly granted. Landes also met with Alton Leonard, president of Puget Power, to discuss reducing the annual bond payments and extending the payback period. Landes believed that a rehabilitated street railway, with new streetcars and rebuilt track, would attract additional riders and pull the system out of its downward spiral, but the high bond payments were making this impossible. Leonard, using the Municipal Railway debt as leverage, insisted on concessions in the company's relationship with City Light, which was then in the process of selling bonds for the Skagit Project. The result was an impasse.

Landes ran for reelection in 1928, losing to Frank Edwards, who had avoided the street railway topic during the campaign. In the meantime, pressure grew outside city hall to resolve the perennial Municipal Railway crisis. A citizens' committee formed with representatives from downtown retailers, property owners, and other groups that had a special interest in public transportation. Headed by hardware store owner Fred Ernst and assisted by graduate students at the University of Washington, the "Traffic Research Commission" organized and funded a study of the Seattle Municipal Railway. The results were presented to Mayor Edwards in January 1929. The commission recommended that the purchase contract with Puget Power be extended from twenty to thirty years and that the city seek legislative authorization in the upcoming session to enact a property tax for support of the Municipal Railway, subject to voter approval. With stable funding, the railway would buy two hundred new streetcars, construct streetcar line extensions, acquire the Rainier Valley line, and rebuild deteriorating track. Most ambitious of all was a long-term proposal to construct two streetcar subways: along the Pike–Pine corridor between Westlake Avenue and Broadway, and underneath the Lake Washington Ship Canal at Fremont. It was no coincidence that streetcar volumes at these locations were the highest in the system, together with the longest service delays.

The *Seattle Daily Times* editorialized that the city council had done nothing to solve the railway's debt problem, to acquire new streetcars, or to make needed route extensions. It pointed out that an independent body, the Traffic Research Commission, had at least come up with some ideas for solving the railway's financial problems and increasing ridership.[4]

The state legislature approved a bill authorizing a city

vote on the property tax proposed by the commission. However, Edwards wanted to use most of the revenue to pay off the purchase bond immediately instead of issuing payments over thirty years, thus postponing badly needed maintenance and capital improvements. This prompted an outcry from the daily *Seattle Star* over the proposed property tax, and the public vote never occurred, a reminder of the lingering resentment toward the "Eastern Capitalists" and the inflated price the city paid for the Puget Power properties.

At a meeting with Leonard in Boston, Edwards did succeed in negotiating a two-year moratorium on bond payments, which was approved by the city council in December 1929.

The Great Depression:
Struggle for Survival

In early 1930 there was a feeling of optimism at the Seattle Municipal Railway. Genuine progress had been made during the previous decade to make the system more efficient, primarily by streamlining routes, converting to one-man cars, and abandoning unproductive lines. The system had avoided deep service cuts. Two promising streetcar route extensions were on the drawing boards. Perhaps most important, the Municipal Railway got a breather in its annual bond payment crisis due to the two-year payment moratorium agreed to by Mayor Frank Edwards and Puget Power.

The optimism was short-lived. As the effects of the Great Depression fully set in, ridership plummeted from 89 million passengers in 1929 to fewer than 60 million in 1933. Fare revenue followed suit, dropping from $5.6 million to $3.7 million. But in 1930 no one knew how bad it would get. Some pundits wrote that this was just a temporary economic bump and repeated the catchphrase "Prosperity is just around the corner."

To take advantage of the extra time allowed by the bond payment moratorium, Mayor Edwards appointed his own committee to study the railway and propose steps to put it on a stable financial footing. The committee released its report in October 1930, and it was not in the least upbeat. In response to accusations that political pressures had impaired sound business practices, the report recommended that the superintendent of railways be selected through the civil service process and that an independent commission be appointed to manage the system, removing governance from the mayor and city council. The committee also recommended that the city's general fund be used to provide collateral for financing needed capital improvements. In a statement prophetic of future controversies, the committee stated that,

> as to the Municipal Street Railway, the mayor's Transit Committee reported in October that unlike the situation when the railway had a virtual transportation monopoly, there was now competition from 90,000 automobiles and 400 taxis. This resulted in loading the cost of operation upon the shoulders of those who could least afford it, the patrons, while using the general fund to make improvements that benefited the competing automobile transportation. "In the nature of the public utility business it is impossible to repay capital costs...without direct assistance from outside sources." It continued, claiming that political pressures had obstructed operations on the basis of sound business practices, and reminded the mayor that wages were the highest on the Coast. It concluded that the system, while given reprieve by the recent moratorium, was really "insolvent". For this reason the general fund must be tapped and operation must be by a commission that was free of political influence.[1]

Following considerable debate, the city council appointed a five-member transit board in September 1931 to manage the Municipal Railway on an "advisory" basis, since giving up its governing role was not authorized by the city charter. The board, under chairman J. W. Maxwell, hired Walter M. Brown as interim superintendent for ninety days. Brown took a leave of absence from his position as manager of the Seattle and Rainier Valley Railway (formerly the Seattle Renton and Southern). During this period, Brown proposed a series of service cuts and reductions of employee pay time. Most of the service cuts were not implemented or were short-lived, but employee shifts were cut significantly, particularly for maintenance staff. In the meantime the council placed three charter amendments on the March 1932 ballot to permanently authorize the commission, abolish the position of superintendent of public utilities, and use the civil service system to select the superintendent of railways. Puget Power, perhaps sensing that something positive would come from this reorganization, granted another one-year moratorium on the bond payments.

The idea of an independent governing body not under the direct control of elected officials was too radical for most citizens at the time, and voters turned down the commission proposal. However, the amendment to abolish the superintendent of public utilities position and use the civil service process to select the superintendent of railways was approved.

A New Superintendent

Using the civil service system, the city selected a new superintendent of railways in early 1934: Albert E. Pierce, a Municipal Railway veteran. Born in Perry, Iowa, in 1888, Pierce received a civil engineering degree from the Lewis Institute of Technology in Chicago. He worked as a survey engineer for the Chicago, Milwaukee, St. Paul and Pacific Railroad between 1907 and 1912, a period when the railroad was extending its main line to the Pacific Northwest and building many branch lines in Washington State. Joining the Army in 1917, Pierce served in France during World War I, achieving the rank of first lieutenant. He started with the Municipal Railway in 1920 and advanced to the position of superintendent of maintenance by 1927. He was acting superintendent of railways on several occasions in the early 1930s.

Pierce's predecessors had included political appointees with little or no railway experience and temporary experts such as Walter Brown who did not have enough time to make their mark. Albert E. Pierce, the last superintendent of the Municipal Railway, would stay on until Seattle's public transit system was on firm financial ground.

The Last Streetcar Extensions

The economic gloom of the early 1930s was overshadowed briefly by the opening of two new streetcar line extensions. On January 31, 1931, the Route 12/Jefferson Park line was extended along Beacon Avenue from Spokane Street to Graham Street, a distance of 1.8 miles. The railway economized by constructing the extension as single track with two passing sidings, and rails were laid in the undeveloped median strip of Beacon Avenue, requiring no paving. The extension replaced a segment of the Beacon Avenue shuttle bus and provided through service to downtown for residents of South Beacon Hill.

The Route 19/Sixth Avenue NW–West Woodland streetcar used a circuitous single-track route on residential side streets north of Leary Way. It ended at NW Sixty-Fifth Street, well short of the city limits, and the track was old and in poor condition. Financed by a $96,000 loan from the employee-supported railway maintenance fund, a new double track was constructed on parallel Eighth Avenue NW from Leary Way to NW Eighty-Fifth Street, a distance of just over two miles. Operating on a wide arterial and straight as an arrow, the new line required no additional cars to operate even though it was twenty blocks longer than the old line. Instead of paving the area between the tracks, the Municipal Railway adopted a new technique of laying down premade concrete slabs in a bed of sand. This was less expensive than conventional paving and allowed easy removal of the slabs for track maintenance. The new line retained the old West Woodland route number (19) but was renamed Eighth Avenue NW. It opened as part of a community celebration on August 1, 1931. (See map of Northwest Seattle route changes.)

Streetcar #516 on Route 12/Beacon Avenue in Jefferson Park, circa 1939. *PNRA photo ST-12-018.*

Car #552 southbound on Route 19/Sixth Avenue NW line at Fifth Avenue NW and NW Sixtieth Street, 1920. *PNRA photo WWASMR-019-008.*

Car #716 southbound on new Route 19/Eighth Avenue NW line near NW Seventieth Street, 1940. *PNRA photo WWASMR-019-020.*

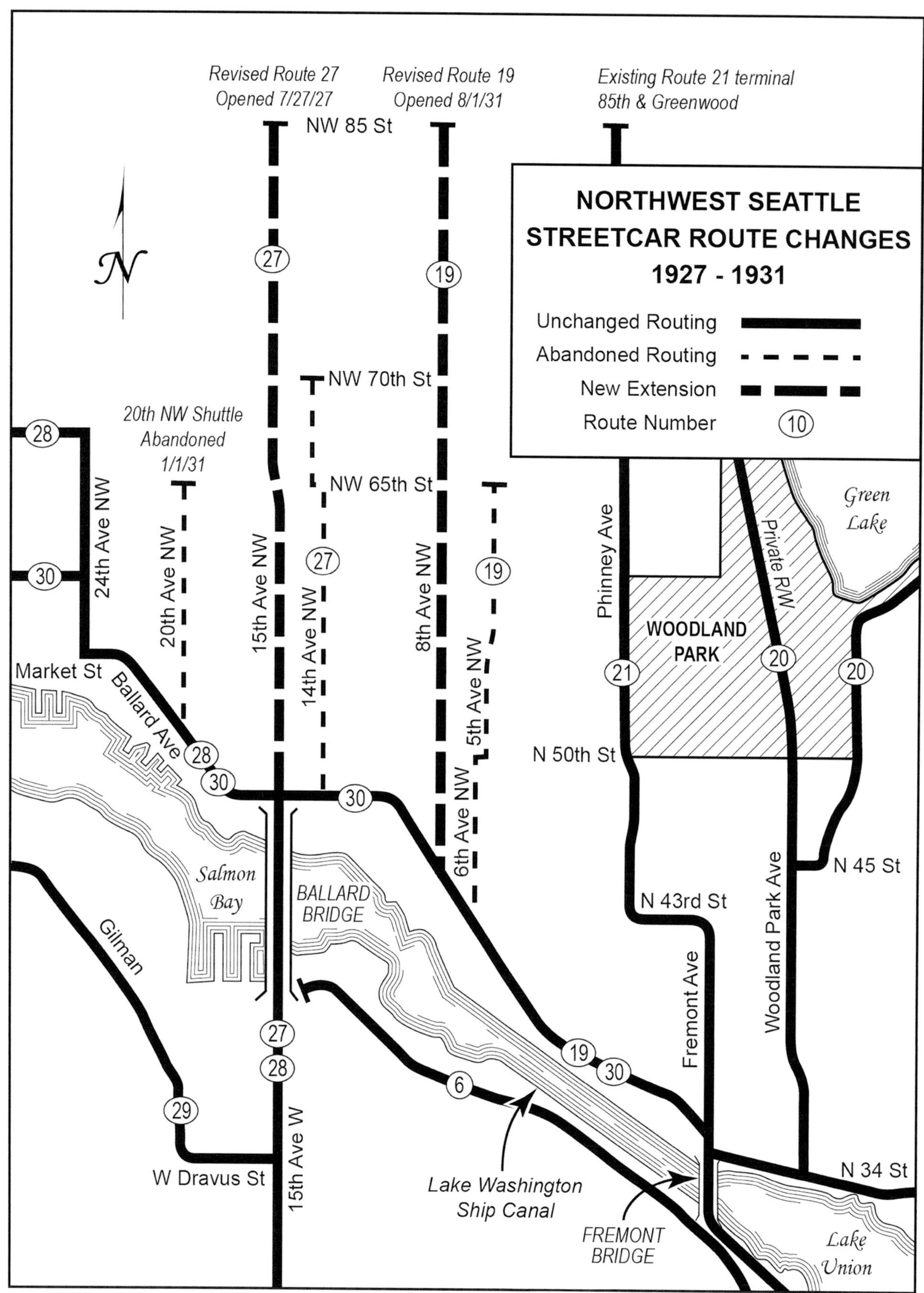

Northwest Seattle Streetcar Route Changes, 1927–1931. *Map by Dave Cooley.*

The End of the Highland Park and Lake Burien Line

Toward the end of the 1920s, increasing auto ownership and the advent of private bus lines south of the city had a major impact on Route 4, the former Highland Park and Lake Burien Railroad. From a high of almost 2 million passengers in 1926, ridership on Route 4 dropped to 1.2 million in 1930. On July 15, 1931, Route 4 service was discontinued between White Center and Seahurst, a distance of 4.5 miles. Residents south of the city limits did not vote in Seattle elections, so there was little political capital to be lost with abandonment of this section. Service remained unchanged between White Center and downtown Seattle until November 1933, when a landslide destroyed a 1.5-mile section of track between Highland Park and West Marginal Way, similar to the 1912 disaster that ended private ownership of the line. Streetcar 357, stuck on the southern section, briefly operated as a shuttle between the slide and White Center, connecting there with the Delridge Way bus, while streetcar service continued in the sparsely populated West Marginal Way area. Ridership dwindled to 170,000 passengers in 1934. This was an unsatisfactory arrangement that could not last.

Superintendent Pierce proposed to restore through streetcar service to downtown by constructing new single track on the steep Highland Park Way hill and connecting it to the "Boeing Spur," a former freight-only track that served the original Boeing airplane factory on West Marginal Way. But a temporary Highland Park bus route initiated several months after the slide proved to be permanent. The short West Marginal Way streetcar segment, the last surviving segment of the Highland Park and Lake Burien Railroad, lasted until December 19, 1937, when it, too, was abandoned.

The Loop Plan

The conversion from two-man to one-man streetcar operation was finally completed in June 1932 except for the cable cars, which remained two-man under an

Work crew removing slide debris on West Marginal Way with streetcar in distance, 1933. *PNRA photo WWAHP-056.*

executive order from newly elected mayor John F. Dore. But more economies were clearly needed. By 1934, fare revenue, once sufficient to cover day-to-day operating expenses if nothing else, fell to the point where out-of-pocket losses exceeded $100,000 for the first six months of the year. Superintendent Pierce and his staff studied the system intently for every possible way to economize. Most service planning efforts focused on reducing route duplication, where two or more lines shared the same path, rather than outright abandonment of service coverage.

In this vein, the most ambitious economy move proposed by Superintendent Pierce was the "Loop Plan" for downtown Seattle. The Loop Plan was intended to end service duplication through downtown once and for all by terminating all streetcar routes in a two-block area roughly bounded by Pike and Pine Streets and Second and Third Avenues. All routes would come together in this area, and no routes would operate the full length of downtown. A passenger arriving downtown from Queen Anne, for example, would need to change to another streetcar to reach the King Street Station. To Pierce, the transfer requirement was a reasonable alternative to major service reductions or even complete abandonment of some lines. In a widely circulated brochure distributed by the Municipal Railway, it was claimed that the savings in car miles and platform hours with the Loop Plan would eliminate the operating deficit and even produce a surplus that could be used to buy new streetcars.

To make the concept operational, several new track curves and switches were installed in the area bounded by Pike and Pine Streets so that streetcars could reverse direction by looping around the block. This work was expensive and disruptive but was completed by August 12, 1934, the first day of the Loop Plan. (See map of 1934 Downtown Loop Plan.)

The plan proved to be a major disappointment. With large volumes of streetcars making 90-degree turns in the center of downtown, traffic was extremely congested and service was routinely delayed, canceling much of the hoped-for savings in platform hours. Waiting streetcar passengers competed with pedestrians for sidewalk space. For purposes of consistency, former through-routed lines,

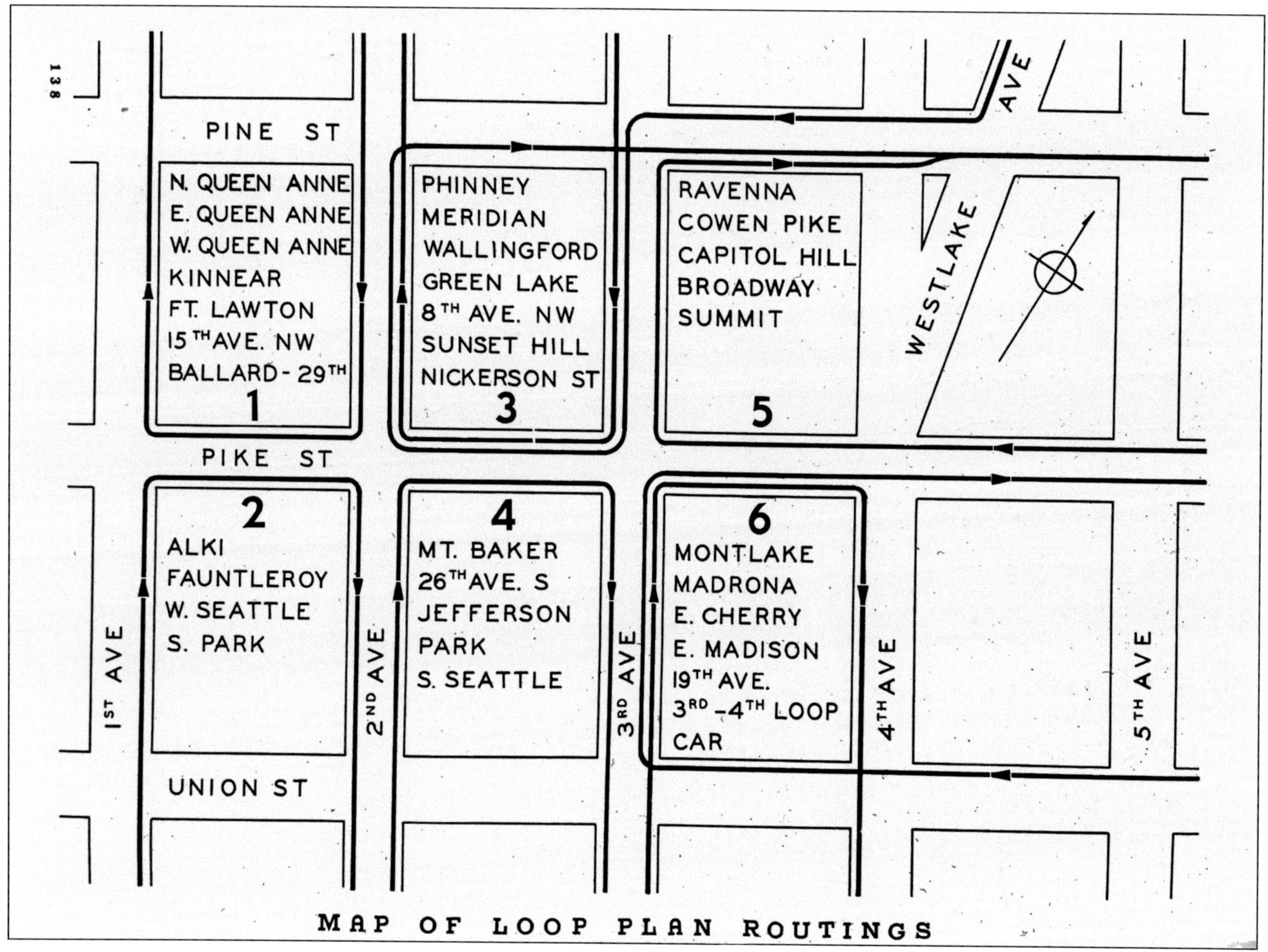

1934 Downtown Loop Plan. *From Seattle Municipal Street Railway brochure. Courtesy of Washington State Archive collection, Puget Sound regional branch.*

such as the Route 12/East Madison–Jefferson Park combination, terminated in the Pine–Pike area along with other routes. The through-routed lines already avoided service duplication, and the Loop Plan did nothing to increase their efficiency. Many passengers complained about the changes, not just because of the transfers required but also because of the rerouting necessary to make the loops work. For example, there was no longer any southbound streetcar service on First Avenue. The experiment ended on December 2, 1934, with all lines returning to their former downtown terminals and through-route hookups.

The First Beeler Plan (1935)

It was time for experienced, out-of-town advice. In late 1934 the city council approved a contract with the Beeler Organization of New York, whose consulting engineer was John A. Beeler, specializing in the finance, engineering, and management of large city transit systems. Beeler had an impressive résumé, starting as a construction supervisor for a Cincinnati cable car line in 1885 and later moving to Colorado, where he oversaw the construction of several streetcar and interurban systems. He founded the Beeler Organization in 1916 and helped prepare appraisals of more than fifty street railways across the country. Beeler also assisted in developing rapid transit plans for several cities, including Boston, Philadelphia, New York, and Cleveland.

Following a comprehensive review of the Seattle Municipal Railway, including a financial analysis and a detailed passenger survey, Beeler delivered his report to the city council on December 10, 1935. It struck a more optimistic tone than the 1931 citizens' committee report. The Beeler plan recommended securing grants and low-interest loans from two New Deal federal agencies, the National Emergency Council and the Reconstruction Finance Corporation, and using these funds to refinance debt, modernize the best streetcars, rehabilitate track and trolley wire and buy new buses to replace the cable lines and some of the electric streetcar lines. The debt would be paid off from increased fare revenue resulting from the modernization, avoiding the need for higher taxes. The plan also called for the establishment of direct express bus service from outlying areas to downtown "at speeds that will compare favorably with the performance of many of the elevated and subway lines in New York, Brooklyn, Boston and Chicago."[2] Here at last was a fairly

Streetcars turning at Second Avenue and Pike Street during the 1934 Loop Plan. *PNRA photo.*

conservative proposal for the Municipal Railway's future that accented the positive, a customer-oriented approach that looked beyond the daily struggle for survival toward a time when the system could offer quality service to an increasing number of patrons.

The 1935 Beeler Plan did not propose abandonment of the streetcar network. While the cable lines would be replaced with motor buses, total electric track mileage would only decrease from 225 miles to 195 miles. Six electric car lines would be converted to buses: Route 1/Fort Lawton, Route 7/Kinnear, Route 10/Montlake, Route 20/Green Lake, Route 24/North Queen Anne, and Route 25/East Queen Anne. Beeler recommended more frequent service provided by modernized cars for the remaining streetcar network. The plan also called for operational changes to speed service. As one example, with the conversion from two-man to one-man streetcars, the loading time for passengers had increased considerably, since only the door nearest to the operator was used for both entry and exit. (With two-man operation, the conductor could operate a separate door.) Beeler proposed that streetcars be equipped with push buttons that let passengers signal the operator for intended stops. He also recommended installation of a separate step-operated exit door.

The release of the 1935 Beeler Plan generated considerable public discussion and media coverage but resulted in few immediate changes at the Municipal Railway. In early 1936 the U.S. Supreme Court held that the National Emergency Council legislation was unconstitutional, so the agency and its programs were abolished. The NEC had been the only New Deal agency that offered grants, as opposed to loans, for rehabilitation of publicly owned utilities.

But at least one recommendation from the 1935 plan was implemented, if only by default. On January 7, 1936, the Fort Lawton line was converted to motor buses, since the replacement for the West Dravus Street Bridge did not include streetcar tracks.

The Second Beeler Plan (1936)

The second Beeler Plan was released in August 1936 and was significantly different from the first plan in both scale and content. The entire rail system would be abandoned, replaced by 240 new trackless trolley coaches and 135 new motor buses. (A few existing motor buses would be retained.) New or rebuilt facilities would be developed to store and maintain the rubber-tired fleet. Lines would be through-routed between the north and south ends of downtown to reduce congestion and duplication of service, and a general network restructuring would streamline routes, increase average speeds, and provide expanded neighborhood route coverage.

Why such a dramatic change from the 1935 Beeler Plan? For one thing, finance options had changed, with no possibility of federal grants. New buses could be acquired from a number of builders on favorable terms, including lease-to-buy and extended payment plans. There were rumors that the Reconstruction Finance Corporation would provide loans only for buses, which later proved unfounded. But most city council members became convinced that only a complete remaking of the system would restore citizen confidence in municipal ownership and start to increase ridership. Trolley coaches and motor buses would provide an entirely new "face" for public transportation in Seattle.

Superintendent Pierce assisted in developing the engineering and facilities section of the new Beeler report while a separate finance team was organized; it consisted of Isaac Commeaux, chief accountant for the city of Seattle; J. D. Ross, superintendent of City Light; and Guy Myers, representing a New York banking syndicate specializing in municipal bonds. They negotiated a tentative agreement with Puget Power to reduce the unpaid amount on the system purchase to $5.2 million in return for an immediate cash settlement. Other elements of the financial plan included $1.2 million to pay the accumulated wage and salary debt and $5.2 million to rehabilitate the system, for a grand total of $11.6 million. To provide this financing, the city council placed a bond issue for this amount on the ballot for the March 1937 civic election. The bond would be payable through increased property taxes spread over ten years.

A group of businesses and neighborhood organizations formed to campaign for the measure, known as Proposition A, and circulated detailed brochures and published newspaper ads backing it. The most publicized event aimed at voter support was a demonstration trackless trolley coach that was loaned to the Municipal Railway by the Twin Coach Company of Kent, Ohio. Temporary double trolley wire was strung along Fourth and Fifth Avenues between the County-City Building and Union Street for the demonstration line, and free public rides began on February 27. The quiet, streamlined trolley coach seemed almost futuristic compared with the city's existing streetcars, and it generated many favorable comments.

Major advances had been made in the design of transit buses by 1937. The truck-based buses of the 1910s and early 1920s had serious shortcomings: ride quality, high step height, low passenger capacity, and poor reliability. By 1937, builders were producing buses designed for passengers from the ground up. Reliability, ride quality,

Twin Coach trolley coach demonstrator at Fifth Avenue and University Street, February 1937 *(Mike Voris collection).*

heating/ventilation, and overall passenger comfort were much improved. Performance and maintainability were also improved with new gasoline and diesel engines designed expressly for bus service. From an economic perspective, perhaps the greatest advance was in passenger capacity. In 1937, transit buses were available with up to forty-four seats, making one-for-one replacement of streetcars with buses possible on all but the most heavily traveled routes.

Similar advances had been made with trackless trolley coaches. Trolley coaches could change lanes when obstructions blocked their way, and they required no tracks or track maintenance. They could use existing streetcar power facilities with some modifications, utilizing the large investment in electrical infrastructure. Trolley coaches also had strong acceleration and good hill-climbing ability and were quiet and free of exhaust fumes. Superintendent Pierce was beginning to reconsider the long-held Municipal Railway position that rubber-tired vehicles were a "lesser" form of mass transit suitable only for neighborhood feeder routes.

Municipal Railway superintendent Albert Pierce with Mrs. Carrie Hatfield, on board Yesler cable car #443 before it was shipped to the Smithsonian in Washington, DC, in October 1937 *(Museum of History and Industry collection).*

During the Proposition A campaign, Mayor John F. Dore opposed the measure, claiming it was backed by nefarious individuals who were out to swindle the voters and bankrupt the city. "I'll not stand aside, I'll not be another Ole Hanson!" he declared.[3] He also opposed trackless trolleys, claiming their technology was unproven. The transit measure was linked to simultaneous negotiations taking place between City Light and Puget Power on the city's potential purchase of Puget Power's electric power business in Seattle. Coupled with news that an associate of a New York banking syndicate had helped develop the financing plan, this increased suspicions that corporate interests were behind a backroom bribery deal involving the Proposition A bonds.

Mayor John F. Dore. *Courtesy of the Seattle Municipal Archives, item 12288.*

Mayor Dore received backing in his opposition from some neighborhood groups and Local 587 of the Amalgamated Transit Union, which supported a rehabilitated streetcar system using modern, streamlined cars. The Presidents' Conference Committee (PCC) streetcar had been introduced in Pittsburgh the previous year and was receiving positive reviews in several U.S. and Canadian cities.

In the March 6 election, Dore got his wish: Proposition A lost by a vote of 39,069 to 53,501. The defeat must have been discouraging to Superintendent Pierce and others who had tired of the seemingly endless series of street railway financial woes.

While Seattle streetcars had been spared, the system was increasingly run-down and destitute. Once again, the Municipal Railway began issuing warrants rather than paychecks to employees. (It should be noted that other city departments also adopted this practice, since the city budget had a $6 million deficit in 1937.) Pierce received authorization from the city council's utilities committee to dismantle some cars for parts to keep the active fleet running, with the body shells sold for scrap. Out-of-service freight cars and electric locomotives were also sold, with one locomotive going to City Light's Skagit River Railway. Maintenance was cut drastically. The Georgetown shops went to one shift per day and a five-day workweek, resulting in a backup of needed overhauls and other major work. Repainting streetcars ceased except when collision damage occurred, and the cars grew faded and shabby. The newest streetcars on the property had been delivered in 1919, and the oldest cars, built in 1898, had been acquired secondhand from Minneapolis and New York City. While streetcars were well known for ruggedness and longevity, most of the Municipal Railway fleet was nearing the end of its useful life.

Superintendent Pierce also was concerned with the Municipal Railway's aging buses. Complaint letters from customers cited instances in which drivers routinely had to use a combination of low gear, hand brakes, and regular service brakes to maintain control of their buses on downhill grades. Naturally, this frightened passengers. In 1936 there were still thirty buses in operation that were delivered between 1920 and 1926, and no new buses had been purchased since 1931. Overall, vehicles in the fleet averaged 354,000 miles of service each, extremely high for motor vehicles of the time. The oldest buses were functionally obsolete and could not keep up with modern traffic. New buses were desperately needed to replace them.

The End of the Seattle and Rainier Valley Railway

While the second Beeler Plan was under development in mid-1936, Superintendent Pierce became involved in discussions about the future of the Seattle and Rainier Valley Railway, the last privately owned streetcar company in Seattle. Formerly known as the Seattle Renton and Southern Railway, the company's franchise had expired in 1934, and the city council had granted two one-year extensions. City council member Roy Misener was concerned that the company would go out of business and leave most of Rainier Valley without service of any kind. In a letter to the city council, Pierce suggested that the city purchase some of the company's assets, including the power supply substation and all track within the city limits. The S&RV's streetcars and Hudson Street carbarn would not be needed, he noted, since the Municipal Railway had surplus cars and could operate the service out of its existing facilities. Overall, he concluded that the purchase would be less costly than acquiring a fleet of new buses to replace the streetcars.[4]

Acting cautiously, the council appropriated funds for a comprehensive appraisal of the company's assets, which was conducted by Beeler and the Seattle Real Estate Board. The company's estimated value, including the carbarn and rolling stock, came to only $357,000.

Seattle and Rainier Valley streetcar #111 at Fourth Avenue and Stewart Street terminal in downtown Seattle, 1933. *PNRA photo WWASRV-003.*

Seattle and Rainier Valley streetcar #103 operating along Lake Washington shoreline between Renton and Rainier Beach, May 1936. *PNRA photo WWASRV-095.*

Seattle Municipal Railway Twin Coach bus #1807, one of the leased buses that replaced Seattle and Rainier Valley streetcar service in 1937, on Dexter Avenue near Halladay Street. *PNRA photo WWASMR-BUS-1807-001 (Mike Voris collection).*

Streetcar derailment at Avalon Way and Spokane Street, January 1937. *PNRA photo WWASMR-02-069 (Museum of History and Industry collection).*

However, by this time the second Beeler Plan had been released. It recommended replacement of all rail service with rubber-tired vehicles. If the plan had any chance of approval, the city would have no logical reason to acquire another streetcar property.

To avoid a large up-front capital expense, Pierce made arrangements to lease twenty-seven new Twin Coach motor buses for service on Rainier Avenue, and Seattle and Rainier Valley streetcars made their last runs on January 1, 1937. Seattle City Light ended up purchasing the company's carbarn and electrical substation.[5]

Fatal Streetcar Crash

A week after the abandonment of the Seattle and Rainier Valley, the worst streetcar accident in Municipal Railway history took place when a West Seattle car went out of control on the Avalon Way hill and failed to make a 90-degree curve east to Spokane Street. Two people died at the scene and twenty-three required hospitalization. Based on reports in the *Seattle Daily Times*, operator Roy Gassett said that the air brakes "froze" and became unresponsive near the top of the hill at Avalon Way and Genesee Street, keeping him from slowing the car as it approached the curve. There wasn't enough time to use the manual brake, which was engaged by spinning a large brass wheel. Instead, Gassett put the car in reverse, which slowed it somewhat, but he estimated the speed at between 15 and 20 miles per hour as he started around the curve. The car body separated from its trucks, turned over, and struck a concrete pillar supporting the Admiral Way overpass.[6]

The subsequent investigation was not conclusive, in part because key pieces of the streetcar were so heavily damaged in the crash. Some proponents of Proposition A pointed to the incident as evidence that the Municipal Railway was so dilapidated that it posed a menace to public safety. The tragedy resulted in a comprehensive review of all Municipal Railway maintenance and operations practices.

More Streetcar Abandonments

Throughout Seattle, major changes were happening with bridges and highways during the late 1930s. In the South End, the Route 5/South Park streetcar line crossed the Union Pacific Railroad yard on a wooden trestle parallel to First Avenue South, and the State Highway Department wanted the trestle right-of-way for a new, wider First Avenue South highway bridge. The department also wanted the Municipal Railway to relocate its tracks on East Marginal Way to make way for street widening. On December 8, 1935, streetcar service was discontinued on First Avenue South between Spokane Street and East Marginal Way, and on East Marginal as far east as Eighth Avenue South. To continue service to South Park, the Route 6/South Seattle streetcar was extended from its terminal at Carleton Avenue and East Marginal Way to South Park over the Eighth Avenue South Bridge. This arrangement lasted only about seven months, as the bridge was closed to streetcars on June 15, 1936, due to structural deterioration. The South Seattle line then returned to its former terminal at Carleton and Marginal Way. Shortly after, a new South Park bus

Route 5/South Park streetcar northbound on First Avenue South near Spokane Street, 1931. Note crossing diamond with Northern Pacific Railway. *PNRA photo WWASMR-005-004.*

line was initiated that served First Avenue South and East Marginal Way and reached South Park using the relatively new Fourteenth Avenue South bascule bridge, which was constructed by King County.

The George Washington Memorial Bridge (also known as the Aurora Bridge) opened in 1932, and State Route 99 was completed as a semi-limited access highway between northern Seattle and downtown a few years later, providing a speedy thoroughfare for motor vehicles. The new bridge and highway stood in stark contrast to Municipal Railway streetcars, which were frequently delayed by Fremont Bridge openings and traffic congestion on Westlake Avenue.

The Route 20/Green Lake streetcar route was the oldest serving Seattle's north end, dating from 1891. The line was scenic, with extensive private right-of-way along the Green Lake shoreline and through Woodland Park. But once again a highway project threatened a Municipal Railway streetcar line. The Green Lake line crossed Highway 99 on a timber trestle at the north end of Woodland Park, and it was in the way of a new bridge where North Sixty-Third Street would pass under Highway 99. While riders appreciated the beautiful vistas from the streetcar, there was no question that bus or trolley coach service from the neighborhood to downtown via Highway 99 would be more direct and much faster.

The city council determined that the Green Lake line would be an ideal test bed for the trolley coach. Ordinance 66294, approved by the council on May 11, 1936, authorized the Municipal Railway to call for bids to purchase twelve new trolley coaches, to be financed with "utility warrants" payable from the railway's earnings. The contract was advertised on July 8, 1936, and four companies submitted bids: Twin Coach, Pullman-Standard, Mack, and St. Louis Car. The city did not respond to the bids and instead elected to wait for the results of

Route 20/Green Lake streetcar #754 passing under dismantled stone pedestrian bridge in Woodland Park, 1935. *PNRA photo WWASMR-20-042.*

the March 1937 referendum on the second Beeler Plan, which was turned down by the voters.[7]

But the Municipal Railway could not stand in the way of a major highway project. The railway initiated motor bus service between downtown and Green Lake on April 27, 1937, using State Route 99 and making a two-way loop around the lake. The Green Lake streetcar ceased operations on May 5. The buses were new twenty-five-passenger Ford Transits equipped with V-8 gasoline engines, less expensive vehicles than the large-capacity trolley coaches the city council had wanted.

In the big picture, the city council fully supported these new bridges and highways, and Superintendent Pierce must have been under enormous pressure to make way for them. It was becoming clear that forces apart from finances were hastening the demise of the streetcar network.

Arthur B. Langlie

During his tenure as mayor, John F. Dore had shown little leadership in addressing the Municipal Railway's problems. He often micromanaged the department, vetoing even small changes that Pierce proposed to save money. Dore opposed any change in governance that would remove the mayor from day-to-day operating decisions. His opposition to Proposition A was instrumental in the defeat of that initiative, yet he did not propose viable alternatives.

City council member Arthur B. Langlie, who had supported Proposition A, ran for mayor in the February 1938 primary election. Incumbent Dore finished third, and in the runoff Langlie defeated Lieutenant Governor Victor A. Meyers, 80,149 votes to 48,563.

Mayor Langlie quickly revived the 1936 Beeler Plan, stating that total rehabilitation and modernization of the city's public transit system was essential. The major point of departure was a new approach to financing. Instead of a bond issue requiring voter approval, modernization would be funded entirely by a Reconstruction Finance Corporation loan that would be paid from increased fare revenue. Federal RFC loans were intended for private companies and public agencies building major infrastructure projects. They required little collateral and had interest rates that were low even by Depression-era standards. The objective was to get the economy moving and provide jobs. To this end, the application process required a borrower to document how the project would stimulate local business and generate employment.

Beeler felt that the new finance plan was viable, based on his experience with Portland, Indianapolis, and other similar-sized cities where transit modernization had been implemented. With the proposed route changes, he projected that service would be speeded up considerably. Since most costs were time related, an increase in speed would decrease platform hour costs while attracting new passengers, a winning combination that would significantly increase the system's net earnings.

Langlie sent former city accountant Isaac Commeaux to Washington, DC, for discussions with the RFC. In September 1938, the agency agreed to loan the city $10 million, of which $4.3 million would be set aside to pay off the bonded debt, leaving $5.7 million available for modernization. As a condition of the loan, the RFC stipulated that management of the department be conducted by an appointed board or commission rather than by the mayor and city council. Early in the 1939 session, the state legislature approved a bill allowing this change in governance.

Langlie also reopened negotiations with Puget Power. The mayor insisted that City Light's proposed purchase of Puget Power's business in Seattle be totally separated from the street railway issue. (City Light superintendent J. D. Ross had pushed to have the agreements bundled together.) The balance remaining on the 1919 purchase totaled $8.3 million, but Puget Power agreed to a cash settlement of just $3.25 million. The stranglehold of the bond payments would soon be gone.[8]

Mayor Arthur B. Langlie. *Courtesy of the Seattle Municipal Archives, item 12290.*

The Great Conversion

As detailed plans for modernization and refinancing began to take shape during the first half of 1939, virtually no service changes were made at the Seattle Municipal Railway. One major exception was in Ballard. The city moved ahead on a plan to replace the wooden approaches to the Ballard Bridge with a new concrete-and-steel structure, requiring the bridge to be closed for an extended period. Starting on May 29, 1939, streetcar Routes 27 and 28 were shifted to the Fremont Bridge instead of the Ballard Bridge to reach downtown, and Route 30/Sunset Hill became a motor bus shuttle. A temporary streetcar line, using the former Fort Lawton route number 29, began service between the south end of the Ballard Bridge and downtown, replacing Route 27 and 28 service through Interbay. On June 30, Route 27 streetcars were replaced by motor buses that connected with Route 28 streetcars at Fifteenth Avenue NW and Ballard Way.

These changes became a dress rehearsal for the massive service restructuring that would start the following year.[1]

On August 1, 1939, the Seattle Municipal Railway officially became the Seattle Transit System. Mayor Arthur B. Langlie appointed three local businessmen to the first transit commission: William F. Paddock,

Route 27/Fifteenth Avenue NW streetcar #739 on reroute via downtown Fremont due to Ballard Bridge closure, 1939. *PNRA photo WWASMR-027-011.*

Route 28 streetcar #717 meeting Fifteenth Avenue NW bus #318 at Fifteenth Avenue NW and Ballard Way during Ballard Bridge closure, 1940. *PNRA photo WWASMR-028-039.*

Evro M. Becket, and Donald H. Yates. Yates served as the initial chair. Under terms of the 1939 authorizing legislation, when a vacancy occurred on the commission, the remaining two commissioners would appoint a replacement; no elected officials would be involved. This somewhat antidemocratic arrangement lasted until 1952, when the RFC loan was paid off. The commission hired Marmion D. Mills, an experienced transportation engineer and consultant, as general manager. Albert Pierce stayed on to assist Mills during the conversion.

While the name had changed, Seattle Transit was still largely a streetcar operation in 1939. Apart from the Seattle and Rainier Valley Railway, only a handful of minor lines had been abandoned during the 1930s, and streetcars continued to provide service on the busiest, most important routes in the city. All of this would change in 1940.

The Final Beeler Plan (1939)

The third and final Beeler Plan was released on August 31, 1939. While it reflected the basic recommendations of the 1936 report, it provided a more detailed operational plan that included refinements to cost estimates and fleet requirements. The new system would now require 235 trolley coaches and 130 motor buses to operate, down from 240 and 135, respectively. To estimate financial results, the plan made assumptions about the timing of the streetcar-to-bus conversions but provided no direction on how to implement them. There were also no details on the new bus storage and maintenance facilities that were needed.

In the plan's cover letter to the mayor and city council, Beeler expressed his usual optimism for the future: "In our opinion, the plan will provide the City with a modern, self-supporting transportation system in con-

New, locally assembled Pacific Car and Foundry Brill trolley coach #776 by Jefferson carbarn, December 15, 1940. *Seattle Transit photo, Mike Voris collection.*

New Kenworth buses parked at Fremont carbarn, 1940. *PNRA photo WWASMR-BUS-303-001.*

Eastbound Madison cable car boarding passengers at Third Avenue, 1940. *PNRA photo WWASMR-MA-008.*

trast to the present one which is a burden financially and so obsolete that it is a detriment to the growth and prosperity of the City."[2]

A Massive Changeover

During the latter half of 1939, new motor buses and trolley coaches were ordered, and engineering plans were drawn up for the double-wire overhead system required by the trolleys. Details of street-by-street routing and route hookups through downtown were worked out, and a route conversion schedule was developed based on anticipated delivery times of new vehicles and the estimated completion dates of the trolley coach overhead system. An interim agreement with Local 587 of the Amalgamated Transit Union allowed major changes in employee work assignments at times other than regular operator reassignment dates. Without this agreement, the conversions would have taken at least a year longer to complete.

To meet the Reconstruction Finance Corporation mandate to provide local employment, the J. G. Brill Company of Philadelphia agreed to have ninety-nine Brill trolley coaches assembled at the Pacific Car and Foundry plant in Renton. Kenworth, a Seattle firm later to become famous for large trucks, supplied forty new motor buses of their own design.

Streetcar conversions started in earnest in early 1940. The Route 12/East Madison streetcar line was abandoned on January 10, followed by several other central Seattle lines in February. Typically, streetcar lines slated for trolley coach operation were first converted to motor bus lines, then to trolley lines as the overhead wiring and power

View of Jefferson carbarn looking north from Jefferson Street, 1936 *(Mike Voris collection).*

supply system was completed. The Nineteenth Avenue line was the first route to get trolley coach service on April 28. The short James Street cable line was abandoned on February 18, with no replacement. The Madison cable line followed on April 14, with trolley coaches replacing the narrow-gauge cars east of Seventh Avenue.

Abandonments continued through the summer and fall of 1940. On August 9 the historic Yesler cable line—the last cable car line in the United States outside of San Francisco—stopped running. Crowds showed up hoping to take a last ride before motor buses took over. Henry MacLeod, writing in the *Seattle Daily Times* on August 9, 1940, described the last run of his city's once-prized form of transportation:

> Like a prehistoric bug lying in wait for its prey, Old No. 2 crouches on the wooden trestle at the foot of Yesler Way. It is Old No. 2's last day, for in a few hours the Yesler Cable will fold its doors like the Arabs, and a silence will steal its way over a street that has known no respite from the clanking cable line since the first car started September 29, 1888.
>
> From the subterranean cavern beneath the car comes the eery [sic] whirr of the cables and the huge wheels that have made them turn on, and on, endlessly but to no destination—nowhere but in the tunnel under Yesler Way—year after year.... There is a clanging and Old No. 2 springs into action with a jerk and a shudder that rends her ancient orange frame.... At the top of the hill the car stops for a moment while an oiler prods the long spout of the can into the cable slot. A passenger says she has ridden on the cable cars 35 years. She remembers riding out to Leschi to dance when she was a girl. The car jerks and bounces her against an upright, but she seems to disregard this jolt from an old friend. She looks out of the window and says: "Maybe I'll be wearing crepe tomorrow. I hate to see the old cars go."[3]

New Maintenance Facilities—and Some Old Ones

The system conversion required many changes to the storage and maintenance facilities needed by the new motor buses and trolley coaches. The early abandonment of central district streetcar lines allowed the Jefferson carbarn to be converted entirely to trolley coaches. At one point Jefferson housed all 235 trolley coaches that had been ordered for the system changeover. Built in 1908 as a "temporary" carbarn for Alaska-Yukon-Pacific Exposition service, Jefferson would continue as a trolley coach facility until 1984.

The 1906 repair shops at Georgetown, with a transfer table designed for streetcars, would have to be rebuilt extensively to accommodate motor buses and trolley

Seattle Transit Atlantic Terminal looking west from Airport Way, 1944. *PNRA photo WWASMR-ATL-001.*

coaches. It was also several miles south of downtown, requiring considerable "deadhead" mileage to access. The transit commission decided to build a replacement facility on Airport Way at Atlantic Street that would include a central shop, service garage, and administration building. The yard was designed to store up to three hundred trolley coaches and motor buses. This facility, known as Atlantic Terminal, would become the signature project of Seattle Transit. It was efficiently designed and self-contained, including training classrooms, a boardroom for commission meetings, and even a restaurant that was open to the public. In May 1941, Seattle Transit's general offices moved to the Atlantic Terminal from the County-City Building, symbolizing the agency's new status as a semiautonomous public agency.

The North Seattle carbarn, located at Fifth Avenue North and Mercer Street, already accommodated motor buses and would become 100 percent bus after the conversion. The Fremont carbarn, at North Thirty-Fourth Street and Phinney Avenue, was a substantial brick building with a yard that could accommodate up to 150 buses. However, the commission chose to sell this property in favor of the Jefferson carbarn, which was better located for the trolley coach system. One of two surviving Municipal Railway carbarns, Fremont is the home of the Theo Chocolate factory as of this writing.

The transit commission sold the smaller facilities owned by the Seattle Municipal Railway, including the three cable car barns and the Massachusetts Street carbarn, which housed both streetcars and buses.[4]

Rails to Rubber

The conversion process continued unabated into the latter half of 1940. The new approaches to the Ballard Bridge were completed, but there were no streetcar tracks on them. The only transit vehicles to use the bridge in the future would be equipped with rubber tires. By the end of 1940, only four streetcar lines remained. All of them operated from the Fremont carbarn: Route 6/South Seattle–Nickerson, Route 19/Eighth Avenue NW, Route 21/Phinney, and Route 22/Meridian. (See the Seattle Transit system map showing remaining streetcar lines as of December 31, 1940.)

While most of the remaining streetcars were operable, no market existed for them as transit vehicles elsewhere. Other U.S. cities were converting to motor buses, trackless trolley coaches, or modern Presidents' Conference Committee streetcars. Old and obsolete streetcars were unwanted, and all but a handful of Seattle's cars would go for scrap. Cars were stripped of usable items such as fare boxes and dismantled at the Georgetown shops and at Northwest Steel Rolling Mills in Ballard. As the changeover progressed, groups of retired streetcars were moved to these final resting places under their own power.

Work car #414 removing streetcar rails on Eighth Avenue NW near Leary Way, April 28, 1941. *PNRA photo WWASMR-WC-027.*

The Route 6/South Seattle–Nickerson and Route 22/Meridian lines were converted to motor bus in early January 1941, leaving only Route 19/Eighth Avenue NW and Route 21/Phinney operating. The Phinney line succumbed on April 5. The Route 19/Eighth Avenue NW line, the last new streetcar line to be opened in 1931, became the last to operate. At 2:15 a.m. on April 13, 1941, car 708 pulled into the Fremont carbarn after finishing its last run on Route 19. The rails to rubber conversion was complete.

Epilogue

The Japanese bombing of Pearl Harbor occurred on December 7, 1941, bringing the United States into World War II. America's entry into the war had profound impacts on urban transportation. The manufacture of new automobiles was halted in early 1942, and rationing of gasoline and tires followed later that year. These measures were taken to maintain supplies of strategic materials, such as steel and rubber, for the war effort. The federal government took control of the production and distribution of transit vehicles through the Office of Defense Transportation, allocating buses and streetcars to the transit companies that served the largest and most important defense industries.

Streetcars did not require oil, gasoline, or tires, but buses did. Across the United States, plans to abandon city streetcars were put on hold. In Portland, for example, the Bridge Transfer line was converted from buses back to streetcars after Pearl Harbor, since the track and trolley overhead were still in place. The Seattle Transit System did not have this option. The system had pulled out the rails at the Jefferson carbarn and converted the facility entirely to trolley coaches by mid-1940. Similarly, rails at the North Seattle carbarn had been removed to enlarge motor bus maintenance facilities and provide storage and truck parking for the trolley overhead and power division. The Georgetown carbarn was leased to Puget Sound Sheet Metal Works, a Boeing subcontractor, and the Fremont carbarn was sold to the U.S. Army for use as a truck facility. In early 1940 the city of Seattle began removing or paving over abandoned streetcar rails. Clearly the city had burned its proverbial streetcar bridges.

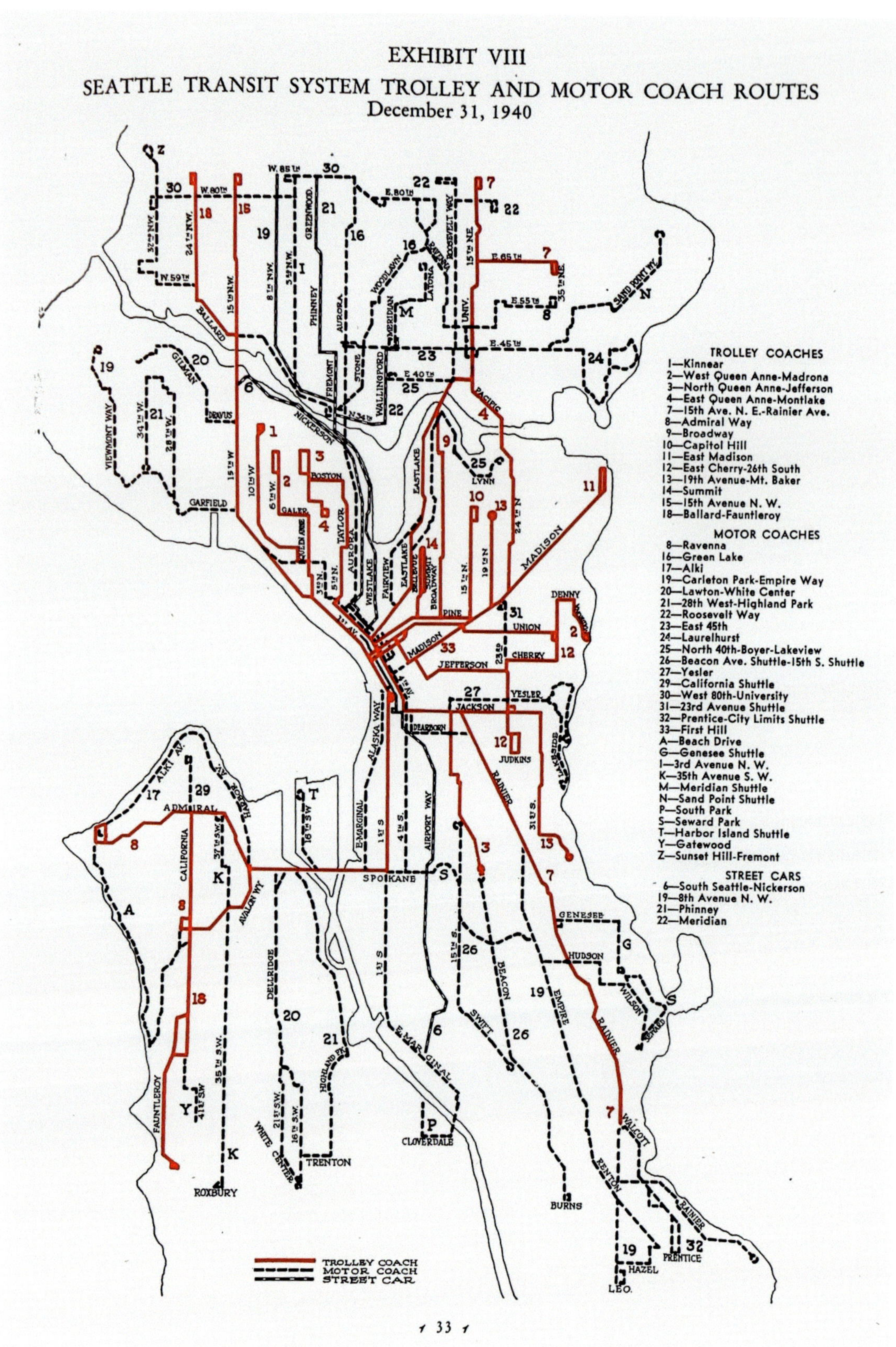

Seattle Transit system map showing remaining streetcar lines as of December 31, 1940, from the Seattle Transit System 1940 Annual Report (*Author's collection*).

As the war intensified, Seattle became an industrial powerhouse, producing ships, aircraft, tanks, and other sophisticated machines for the military. In late 1941, Albert Pierce left Seattle Transit and became the local director of the War Production Board, helping to coordinate defense industries in the Northwest. The population of Seattle increased from 368,000 in 1940 to an estimated 500,000 at the end of 1943. Employment increased from 148,000 to 249,000 during the same period.

The huge increase in population and employment, together with the restrictions on private automobile use, put tremendous pressure on Seattle Transit. Ridership increased from 55 million passengers in 1940 to 115 million in 1943. An all-time high for transit use in Seattle was reached in 1945 with 135 million passengers. The system Beeler had designed was totally unprepared for this level of usage. Buses carried crush loads and routinely passed up waiting passengers. After pleading with the Office of Defense Transportation, Seattle Transit was given authorization to purchase 72 additional trolley coaches and 103 additional motor buses between 1942 and 1945. The system was so desperate for vehicles that it salvaged a 1928 Mack motor bus from a wrecking yard, rebuilt it, and put it back into service. While programs such as staggered work hours and car pool promotions helped, the overcrowding remained severe at least through 1946.

Was the decision to convert entirely from streetcars to rubber-tired transit a wise one? In retrospect, the full conversion was clearly premature, coming at a time when ridership was growing rapidly due to the World War II defense buildup. It was also becoming apparent by 1941 that acquiring more motor buses and trolley coaches would be problematic. The streetcars were obviously a proven technology and could have provided significant extra passenger capacity, particularly on the West Seattle lines serving the Harbor Island shipyards. But despite crush loads and pass-ups, the public generally did not view the streetcar abandonment as a bad decision. To many Seattle residents, streetcars were old-fashioned. A *Seattle Daily Times* reporter observed, "The city will engage in no official weeping for the twenty-seven-year-old street car which made the last run on the last line, nor for any of its fellows which will be presently carted off to the glue factory—in this case the Northwest Steel Rolling Mills, where they are to be junked for scrap."[5] Most Seattle citizens never had the opportunity to experience modern, smooth-riding, streamlined streetcars running on well-maintained track. A few letters to the editor in the local newspapers commented that Seattle Transit had been too hasty in abandoning the streetcars, but this seemed to be the minority view.

The heavy wartime ridership generated more fare revenue than Beeler had predicted, and the Reconstruction Finance Corporation loan was paid off ahead of schedule. The transit commission established a renewal and betterment fund to finance new vehicles and facility improvements, and the entire motor bus fleet was replaced by 1955. Through methodical service reductions and regular fare increases, Seattle Transit remained a self-sustaining city department until 1965, when fare revenues failed to meet operating expenses for the first time. In that year the state legislature approved a bill permitting local governments to subsidize public transit systems on a continuing basis using tax revenue, finally addressing the 1922 Supreme Court decision that had impaired the entire concept of municipal ownership. Today, mass transit is recognized as a vital public service that needs continual support from local taxes.

In the end, the history of the Seattle Municipal Street Railway is a saga of economic hardship, creativity, and perseverance. Saddled almost from the beginning by a huge debt load, declining ridership, and a legal ruling that severely impaired the ability to draw on public money for improvements, the railway department was a political hot potato for ten Seattle mayors. A large city streetcar network requires constant maintenance and renewal. It is a tribute to Municipal Railway employees that they were able to keep the system operating for more than two decades, even during times when they were paid with promissory notes instead of paychecks. Albert Pierce, the final superintendent, diligently sought new ways to provide service at less cost in the face of constant political meddling. Ultimately, public transit in Seattle achieved stability through the leadership of a progressive mayor, Arthur B. Langlie, who overcame the political and financial obstacles that had vexed previous executives. Langlie's success with transit and other civic issues caught the attention of voters statewide, and he was elected governor of Washington in November 1941.

A few remnants of Seattle's original streetcar system still exist. The Fremont streetcar barn was used as a truck garage and then as a brewery and is the home of a chocolate factory as of this writing. The greatly remodeled Madison cable car barn is now part of the campus of Seattle University. Two Yesler cable cars have survived, one at the Smithsonian in Washington, DC, and the other at Seattle's Museum of History & Industry. The body of Seattle Birney streetcar #210 still exists and is owned by the Metro Employees Historic Vehicle Association. At Leschi Park, a concrete overpass used by Yesler cable cars is still in place and is now part of a greenbelt trail. At locations where streetcar rails were paved over rather than removed, worn asphalt often reveals their continued existence until city crews return to pave the area once again.

A lasting legacy of the streetcar era in Seattle is the city's many pedestrian-friendly residential areas and neighborhood business districts—the "streetcar suburbs." Well into the 1920s, residential developers realized that access to public transportation was not just a convenience but also a vital selling point. The result was affordable single-family homes built on small lots with a complete sidewalk network that connected with the nearest streetcar line, often just a five-minute walk away. Streetcar lines also contributed to the prosperity of many neighborhood business districts. Business districts such as Ballard, Wallingford, and West Seattle Junction that developed adjacent to streetcar hubs benefited from the high levels of pedestrian traffic the streetcars generated. Their comfortable scale, pedestrian-friendly sidewalks, and small, independent businesses continue to contribute to the vitality of Seattle's neighborhoods.

Route 28 car #721 eastbound on Market Street in Ballard business district, 1940. *PNRA photo WWASMR-28-035.*

A Tour of Seattle Streetcar Routes

This chapter features a photographic tour of the Seattle streetcar network arranged by route, starting with the three cable car lines. Every route in service during 1935 is pictured. The cable car routes were designated by name only, while the electric streetcar routes were both named and numbered. To provide geographic perspective, the chapter includes a 1935 Seattle Municipal Railway system route map and a map showing details of downtown routing.

Seattle Streetcars: A Primer

To start off the photographic tour, it is helpful to have a basic knowledge of the Municipal Railway streetcar fleet during the 1930s:

Cable Cars: All cable cars were double-ended and reversed direction at a stub-end single track at the end of the lines. The cars were operated by two men (a gripman and a conductor). While electric streetcars used the standard railroad track gauge of 4 feet 8.5 inches between the rails, the cable routes were narrow-gauge line: 3-foot gauge on Yesler, and 3-foot-6-inch gauge on Madison Street and James Street. In the photos, one can see how the cable cars were noticeably smaller than their electric car counterparts. Each cable car line had its own combined powerhouse and carbarn. The Yesler carbarn was located at the eastern end of Yesler Way on the Lake Washington shoreline. The Madison carbarn was on the south side of Madison Street at Eleventh Avenue, and the James carbarn was on the east side of Broadway at James Street. Each of the carbarns had a large electric motor that powered the cable-winding machinery, which was closely monitored during all hours of operation. One unique feature was the use of a small "pusher" electric trolley to move cable cars within the Yesler and Madison carbarns, where cable propulsion would have been impractical. A photo of the Madison pusher is shown on page 78.

Unlike San Francisco's cable cars, all Seattle cable cars were fully enclosed by 1915 due to the colder Northwest climate. The cars had spring-loaded doors that were opened and closed by the conductor.

Electric streetcars: The electric streetcar fleet was made up of both double-end and single-end cars. A double-end car had complete operating controls on each end and doors on both sides, and could reverse direction at the route terminal without a turnaround loop or "wye" track. (A wye was a section of track shaped like a Y that enabled streetcars to reverse direction at a street intersection. Cars entered from the bottom of the Y, went to the upper right hand corner of the intersection, backed into the left hand corner, then pulled forward to the bottom of the Y heading in the opposite direction.) The cars had movable seats that could be changed at the end of the line to face in either direction. Single-end cars had doors on just one side of the car, like a bus. A small control panel at the back end of the car was equipped with power and brake levers, allowing the operator to see where he was going when reversing direction at a turnaround wye. On many of Seattle's single-end streetcars, the back half of the car was partially open to the weather, with a roof but no sides. By 1920, all of these cars had been fully enclosed, but the different window size in the newly enclosed section made them look somewhat awkward and home-built. A photo of one of these cars is shown on page 83.

Seattle streetcar routes were mostly double-tracked (one track for each direction of travel), but some had two-directional single-track sections near the end of the line. These sections were protected by signals that alerted the operator if another streetcar was occupying the track ahead. Most track switches were electrically powered and controlled by the operator with a power-on/power-off relay activated by the controller. All streetcars, including single-end cars, were equipped with a trolley pole on each end. Each trolley pole was topped with a small grooved steel wheel that rolled along the bottom of the round trolley wire for current collection.

After the last electric car route was converted to one-man operation in 1930, the use of small single-truck cars declined. Single-truck "Birney" cars continued to operate on the Twenty-Third Avenue shuttle line and as extras on the Broadway line, but their small capacity

Seattle Municipal Street Railway System, 1935

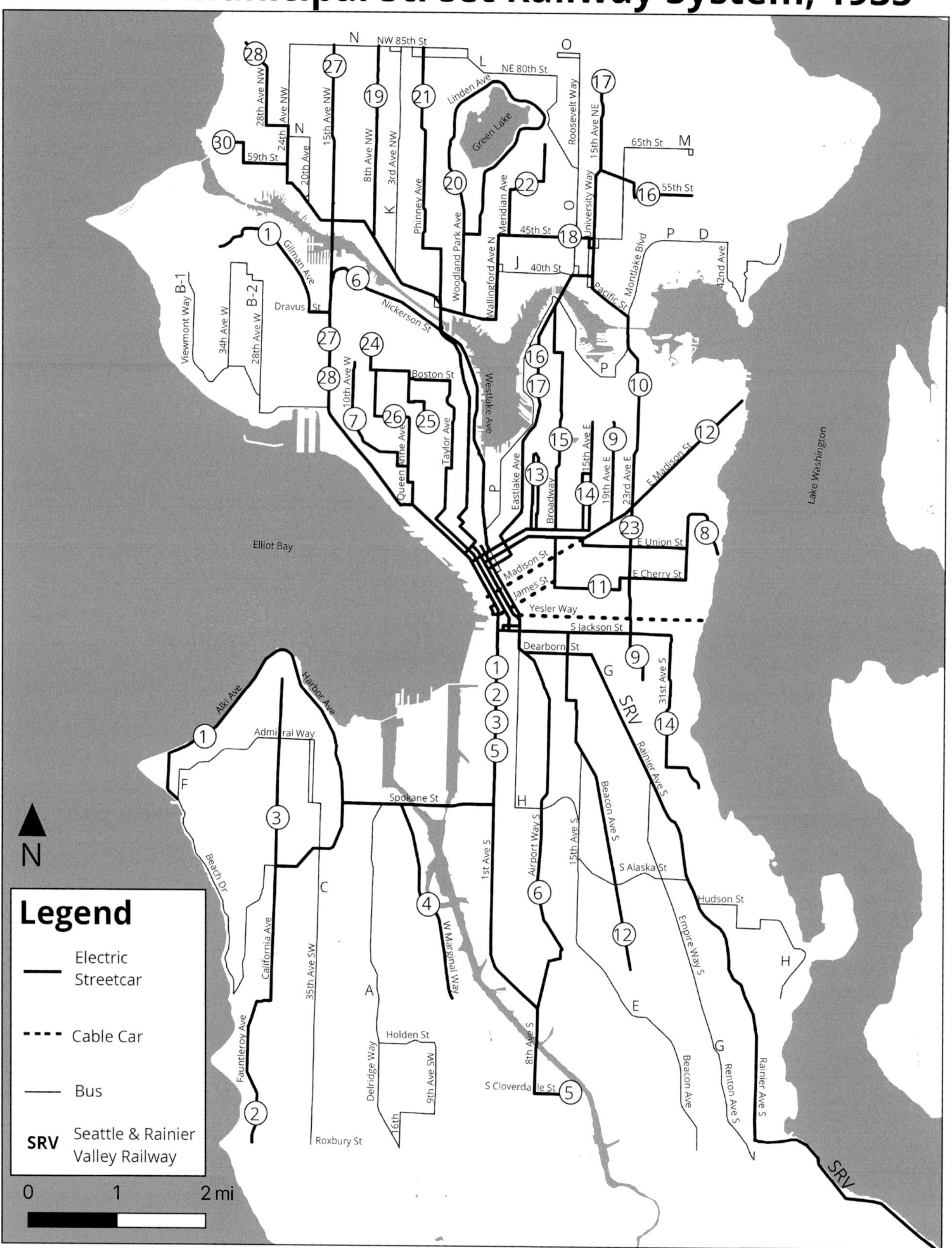

1935 system route map showing all rail and bus routes, including independent Seattle and Rainier Valley Railway. *Map by Sophia Nelson.*

was a major disadvantage on routes that had rush hour ridership surges. A photo of a single-truck Birney on the Twenty-Third Avenue line is shown on page 105.

The Seattle Municipal Railway had an extensive private telephone system, with stations located at all major terminals and at many intermediate points as well. When an operator reached the end terminal, he would call the dispatcher, state his time of arrival, report any operational problems, and receive any special instructions. A photo of an operator reporting in is shown on page 103.

THE RIDING EXPERIENCE, CIRCA 1935

What was it like to ride a Seattle streetcar during the 1930s?

To find where to board, passengers looked for a "Car Stop" sign attached to the overhead trolley span wires. Tracks were located in the middle of the street, so passengers waited on the sidewalk and stepped into the curb traffic lane to board when the streetcar approached. Some stops had small "safety islands" where lane markings diverted traffic around a designated passenger loading area by the tracks.

The wait for a streetcar wasn't long. Even during the height of the Great Depression, most individual streetcar lines ran every ten to fifteen minutes during off-peak periods, and more often during weekday rush hours. The Alki, South Seattle–Nickerson, and Sunset Hill routes had the longest wait, with a car every twenty minutes. At locations where more than one route shared the same track, service was very frequent during all time periods. At Broadway and East Pike Street, for example, five routes converged and there was almost always a streetcar in sight.

Passengers boarded at the front of the streetcar and deposited their fares in a cashbox by the operator. Each fare paid was recorded by a fare register, which rang every time the operator pulled a cord. The adult fare in 1935 was 10 cents cash or three tokens for 25 cents; children rode for 3 cents, and ten tokens cost 25 cents. The operator would give change, sell tokens, and provide a free transfer good for travel on other Municipal Railway streetcars or buses if used within one hour. In addition, Municipal Railway transfers were valid on Seattle and Rainier Valley Railway streetcars and vice versa under an agreement with that company.

Once on board, passengers generally found a seat during off-peak periods. In 1935, standees were largely confined to the rush hour commute and special event times. Passengers faced forward on seats made of either wood or wicker, in contrast to the more comfortable leather or fabric seats found on Presidents' Conference Committee streetcars and contemporary buses. The car would start off with a jerk and would reach a cruising speed of about twenty-five miles per hour. The ride quality and noise levels depended heavily on the maintenance of individual cars and the condition of the track. Unfortunately, the Municipal Railway fell behind in both areas during the 1930s. At its worst, cars would tend to move abruptly back and forth where rails were slightly out of gauge, and loud noises would come from gears, whining traction motors, and worn rail joints. These noises, heard both inside and outside the cars, were particularly loud when going through track switches and crossovers. A well-maintained lightweight streetcar running on good track rode smoothly and created a minimal amount of noise, but this experience had become the exception rather than the rule by the late 1930s.

When passengers approached their destination, they walked to the front of the car and requested the operator to stop. No buzzer or bell was provided to signal the operator, and boarding passengers sometimes had to wait for others to deboard.

Scheduled travel times to various points in the system were generally close to today's bus and trolley coach times—surprising, considering the slow acceleration and limited top speed of the ancient streetcars. In 1935, for example, streetcars took twenty-one minutes to travel from Second and Pike to Fifteenth Avenue East and East Galer Street on Capitol Hill; the current trolley coach running time is twenty-three minutes using virtually the same routing. The Phinney streetcar took thirty-four minutes between Pike Street and Eighty-Fifth and Greenwood; today's Route 5 motor bus time is just five minutes less, despite a seemingly faster routing using Highway 99 instead of the Fremont Bridge.

The quality of Municipal Railway operating employees was outstanding. In consultant John Beeler's 1935 report, he noted: "Scarcely without exception, the operators were careful and alert in negotiating hills and heavily traveled street intersections. We found them to be uniformly courteous and helpful, especially to little children and elderly and blind patrons. As an example, instances were noted where blind patrons leaving the cars were conducted safely to the sidewalk by the operators."[1]

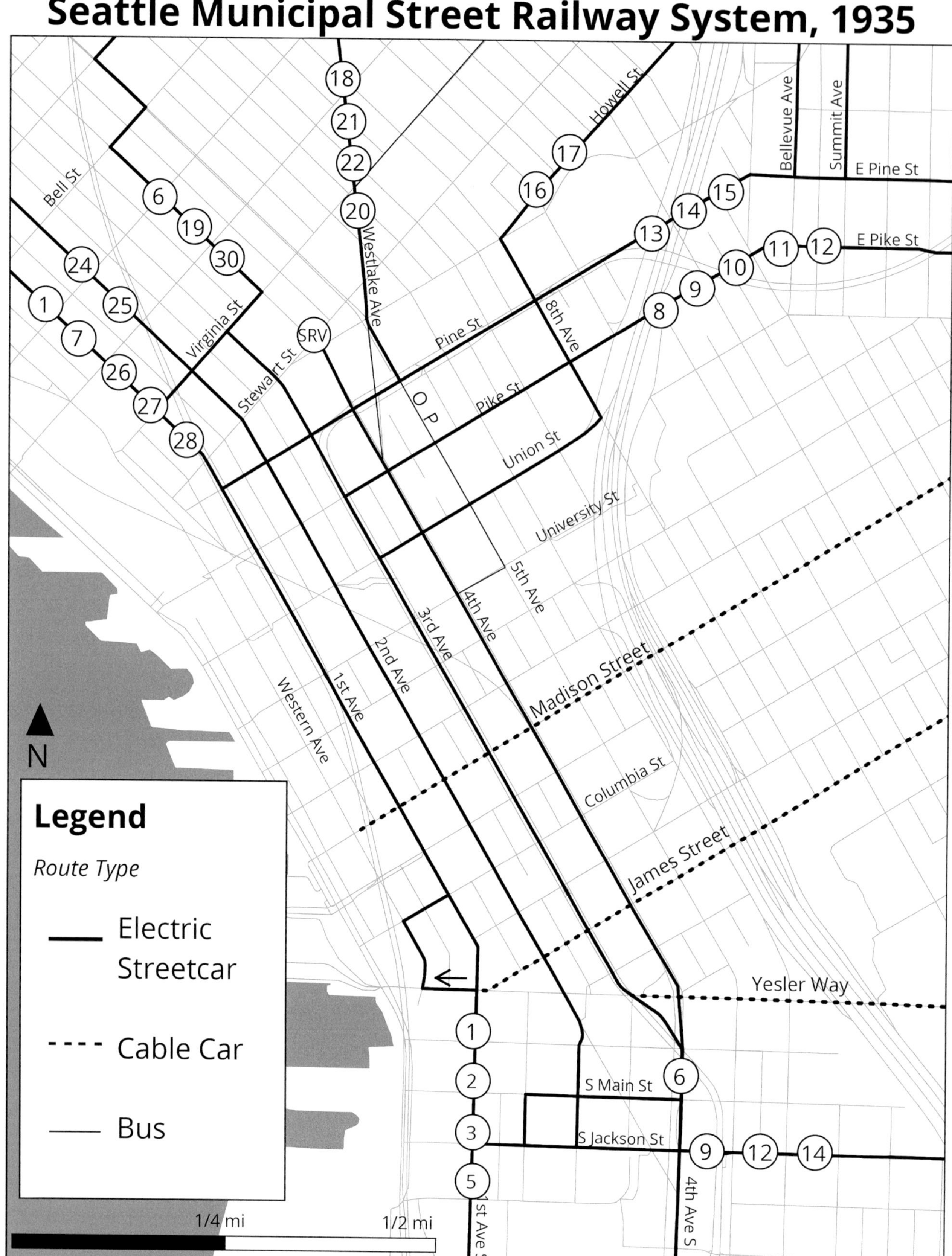

1935 map with detail of downtown Seattle routing. *Map by Sophia Nelson.*

1935 Seattle Municipal Street Railway Streetcar and Bus Routes

Cable Car Routes

Madison Street
James Street
Yesler Way

Electric Streetcar Routes

Route 1, Alki Point–Downtown–Fort Lawton
Route 2, Downtown–Fauntleroy
Route 3, Downtown–West Seattle
Route 4, West Marginal Way
Route 5, Downtown–South Park
Route 6, South Seattle–Downtown–Nickerson
Route 7, Downtown–Kinnear
Route 8, Downtown–Madrona Park
Route 9, Twenty-Sixth Avenue South–Downtown–Nineteenth Avenue
Route 10, Downtown–Montlake
Route 11, Downtown–East Cherry
Route 12, Jefferson Park–Downtown–East Madison
Route 13, Downtown–Summit
Route 14, Mount Baker–Downtown–Capitol Hill
Route 15, Downtown–Broadway
Route 16, Downtown–Ravenna
Route 17, Downtown–Fifteenth Avenue NE
Route 18, Downtown–Wallingford
Route 19, Downtown–Eighth Avenue NW
Route 20, Downtown–Green Lake
Route 21, Downtown–Phinney
Route 22, Downtown–Meridian
Route 23, Twenty-Third Avenue
Route 24, Downtown–North Queen Anne
Route 25, Downtown–East Queen Anne
Route 26, Downtown–West Queen Anne
Route 27, Downtown–Fifteenth Avenue NW
Route 28, Downtown–Ballard–Twenty-Eighth Avenue NW
Route 30, Downtown–Sunset Hill

Motor Bus Routes

Route A, Twenty-Fourth Avenue SW (Delridge Way)
Route B, Carleton Park
Route C, Thirty-Fifth Avenue SW
Route D, Laurelhurst Local
Route E, Beacon Hill
Route F, Admiral–Alki–Beach Drive
Route G, Empire Way (now Martin Luther King Jr. Way)
Route H, Seward Park
Route J, Fairview Local
Route K, Third Avenue NW
Route L, Green Lake–University
Route M, East Sixty-Fifth Street
Route N, West Eighty-Fifth Street
Route O, Fairview Express
Route P, Laurelhurst Express

Cable Car Lines

Madison cable car #57 eastbound at Fourth Avenue and Madison Street, 1911. Car #57 is surrounded by three Seattle landmarks in this scene. *Left*, the Seattle YMCA; *center*, the luxurious Lincoln Hotel, which burned in a spectacular 1920 fire; *right*, the 1906 Carnegie Library. *PNRA Photo WWASMR-MA-010 (Museum of History and Industry collection).*

"Pusher" electric car #406 at Madison cable car barn, Eleventh and Madison, 1940. To move cable cars between the carbarn and the street, the Municipal Railway employed a small narrow-gauge "pusher" car powered by overhead trolley wire, as shown in this rare photo. *PNRA Photo WWASMR-MA-022.*

Madison cable car #61 eastbound between Third and Fourth Avenues, 1935. Looking antique even by 1930s standards, car #61 climbs the 17 percent grade on this section of Madison Street with ease. In the center is the Seattle YMCA and in the distance is the old clock tower of Central School. *PNRA Photo WWASMR-MA-009 (Museum of History and Industry collection).*

Madison cable car #48 westbound between Tenth and Eleventh Avenues, 1938. Car #48 shows the sliding doors and folding steps characteristic of Seattle cable cars after 1915. The doors and steps were interlocked and operated by the conductor. *PNRA Photo WWASMR-MA-015.*

James cable car #73 westbound at Second Avenue and James Street, early 1930s. At twenty-seven feet, the James cable cars were slightly shorter than the Yesler and Madison cars. In this scene, car #73 is passing by the art deco–style Hartford Building. *PNRA Photo WWASMR-JA-006 (Museum of History and Industry collection).*

James cable car #69 westbound at Seventh Avenue, 1940. The James Street line served a neighborhood with an eclectic mix of architectural styles, as seen in this view. *PNRA Photo WWASMR-JA-012 (Museum of History and Industry collection).*

James cable car #69 westbound near Eighth Avenue, 1940. Trinity Parish Episcopal Church, a James Street landmark that has survived, is the backdrop for this view of car #69. *PNRA photo WWASMR-JA-009.*

Yesler cable car #3 approaching outer terminal at Leschi Park, 1940. Yesler was the longest of the three cable lines and had the most spectacular views. The cars descended to the shore of Lake Washington on this elevated structure. The concrete section of this structure still exists and crosses Lake Washington Boulevard with a greenbelt park on the top. *PNRA photo WWASMR-YE-054.*

Yesler cable car #21 westbound at Terrace Street, 1940. As the Yesler line approached its downtown terminal, it went by the old Public Safety Building on Terrace Street. Here, car #21 passes by the building with a 1937 Packard parked at the curb. *PNRA photo WWASMR-YE-045.*

Yesler cable car #2 westbound at Thirty-First Avenue, 1940. Once off the elevated structure, cars entered Yesler Way and stayed on that street until reaching downtown. *PNRA photo WWASMR-YE-048.*

Yesler cable car #20 at Third Avenue and Yesler terminal, 1940. Originally the Yesler line ended at Occidental Avenue in Pioneer Square, but the line was cut back two blocks to Third Avenue in 1920. In this view, an electric streetcar is passing a Yesler car sitting at the Third Avenue terminal. Most of the buildings in this scene still exist, including, *from left to right*, the Frye Hotel, the Smith Tower, the Morrison Hotel, and the King County Courthouse. *PNRA photo WWASMR-YE-040.*

Electric Streetcar Lines

Route 1/Alki car #678 on Harbor Avenue SW between SW Florida Street and Fairmont Avenue SW, 1940. Car #678 passes by a Northern Pacific boxcar and a row of Alaska Steamship Company steamers made surplus by the Depression. *PNRA photo WWASMR-01-015 (Harold Hill, photographer).*

Route 1/Alki cars #527 and #584 passing on Alki Avenue SW near Bonair Drive SW with Elliott Bay on left, 1911. When the Alki line opened in 1907, the track along Alki Avenue was supported on wooden pilings driven into the beach sand, as shown in this early view. Later the city built a seawall and elevated the track and roadway well above the high-tide line. During the summer months the line carried many riders to the beach and to an amusement park at Duwamish Head. *PNRA photo WWASMR-01-021 (Museum of History and Industry collection).*

Route 1/Alki car #686 at Beach Drive and SW Orleans Street turnaround loop, 1939. Single-end car #686 is laying over at the Alki turnaround loop, with a glimpse of Puget Sound in the center of the photo. By 1939 the streetcar fleet was starting to look shabby and run-down after years of deferred maintenance. *PNRA photo WWASMR-01-025 (Harold Hill, photographer).*

Route 2/Fauntleroy car #287 outbound on Fauntleroy Place private right-of-way, 1930. The Fauntleroy line served a lightly populated neighborhood south of Lincoln Park appropriately named "Endolyne." *PNRA photo WWASMR-02-030.*

Route 2/Fauntleroy car #665 southbound at First Avenue and Pike Street, 1940. A Fauntleroy car pauses by the Pike Place Market as a passenger boards. In the background is the Liberty Theatre, an ornate terra-cotta landmark. *PNRA photo WWASMR-02-002.*

Route 3/West Seattle car #581 southbound at First Avenue South near SW Atlantic Street, 1940. After the Railroad Avenue elevated was dismantled in 1929, West Seattle streetcars started using this track between downtown and Spokane Street. Here, car #581 has just crossed the track junction where streetcars could turn into the Atlantic Street carbarn one block west. *PNRA photo WWASMR-03-068 (Museum of History and Industry collection).*

Route 3 cars #314 and #397 passing at Twenty-Sixth Avenue SW and SW Spokane Street, 1940. Two West Seattle streetcars have just passed each other near the west end of the Youngstown streetcar viaduct, built in 1930 to provide streetcar access to the twin Spokane Street bridges over the Duwamish River. *PNRA photo WWASMR-03-070 (E. W. Whinihan, photographer).*

West Seattle car #675 at California Avenue SW and SW Atlantic Street terminal "wye," 1940. The outer terminal for Route 3 was in the Admiral District, where streetcars backed into a wye on Atlantic Street, then pulled forward onto California Avenue for the return trip. The Seattle Municipal Railway telephone box can be seen mounted on the utility pole to the left. *PNRA photo WWASMR-03-40.*

Lake Burien car #110 at Seahurst terminal, SW 152nd Street and Twenty-First Avenue SW, circa 1915. The crew of #110 is posing by their streetcar shortly after the Lake Burien line became part of the Municipal Railway. A real estate office is on the right, and a viewing tower was built nearby to give prospective property buyers a vista of Puget Sound and the surrounding area. *PNRA photo WWAHP-001.*

Route 5/South Park car southbound on First Avenue South at Railroad Way, circa 1918. A trio of streetcars led by a South Park car is about to cross the four steam railroad tracks on Railroad Way. Judging by the male passengers running for the cars, it may be shift change time at the nearby Skinner & Eddy shipyard. The Smith Tower looms in the background. *PNRA photo WWASMR-05-002.*

Route 6/Nickerson car #358 on Dexter Avenue northbound near Halladay Street, 1940. Taken from the Aurora Bridge, this photo shows a Nickerson car descending Queen Anne Hill with Lake Union as a backdrop. Nickerson was the first route built and operated by the Seattle Municipal Railway. *PNRA photo WWASMR-06-001.*

Route 6/South Seattle car #394 on Twelfth Avenue South between Airport Way and South Bailey Street, 1939. This view of car #394 in the Georgetown business district shows the original Rainier brewery in the distance. *PNRA photo WWASMR-06-021.*

Route 7/Kinnear car #384 turning from westbound Mercer Street to northbound Second Avenue West, 1940. The uptown neighborhood served by Route 7 was a mix of apartment buildings and large houses. The Queen Anne Revival–style house pictured here still exists. *PNRA photo WWASMR-07-031 (Harold Hill, photographer).*

Route 8/Madrona car #346 at turnaround loop on Lake Washington, 1940. This scenic streetcar loop served a small amusement park on Lake Washington that later became the city-owned Madrona Park. Madrona trolley coaches continue to loop at a location about two hundred feet north of where car #346 is pictured. *PNRA photo WWASMR-08-011 (Harold Hill, photographer).*

Work car #414 at Madrona streetcar pier, 1921. Adjacent to the Madrona streetcar loop was this pier, used to deliver cable reels to the Yesler cable car powerhouse, located a half mile south on the Lake Washington shoreline. Work car #414, equipped with a crane, has just unloaded a cable reel on a scow, which will be towed to the powerhouse by a tugboat. *PNRA photo WWASMR-WC-023.*

Route 9 car #344 at Twenty-Sixth Avenue South and South Judkins Street turnaround wye, circa 1940. The Rainier Heights neighborhood (later called Judkins Park) developed around this streetcar terminal. In this 1940 scene, a passenger is about to board car #344 after it has just left the west leg of the turnaround wye. After heading downtown on Jackson Street, the car will continue to the north end of Route 9 at Interlaken Park. *PNRA photo WWASMR-09-007 (Harold Hill, photographer).*

Route 9 car #347 at Nineteenth Avenue and Galer Street turnaround wye, 1940. The north end of Route 9 served a prosperous single-family neighborhood on the east side of Capitol Hill. Here, car #347 rests between runs on the west leg of the turnaround wye, with Interlaken Park in the background. *PNRA photo WWASMR-09-003 (Harold Hill, photographer).*

Route 10/Montlake car #392 northbound on Montlake Boulevard at East Hamlin Street approaching the Montlake Bridge, 1940. Montlake streetcars operated through this landscaped median just south of the Montlake Bridge. The median, a legacy of the Olmsted park and boulevard plan, is mostly gone now, replaced by additional traffic lanes. *PNRA photo WWASMR-10-011 (Harold Hill, photographer).*

Route 10/Montlake car #395 westbound on private right-of-way adjacent to NE Pacific Street with University of Washington campus on right, 1940. In this view, a Montlake car is operating on the north side of the university golf course. The university's Forestry Building is on the far right. *PNRA photo WWASMR-10-008 (Harold Hill, photographer).*

Route 11/East Cherry car #502 southbound on Thirty-Fourth Avenue near East Cherry Street, 1940. Route 11 served the Madrona neighborhood at its eastern end, an attractive residential area of large single-family homes. Here, a southbound car is about to turn from Thirty-Fourth Avenue onto East Cherry Street on its way downtown. *PNRA photo WWASMR-11-001 (Harold Hill, photographer).*

Route 11/East Cherry car #501 northbound on Broadway at James Street with cable car #71 on right, 1940. Route 11 made a convenient connection with the James Street cable car at Broadway and James, as shown in this view looking north on Broadway. The cable car barn and powerhouse are on the right. Passengers who stayed on board the East Cherry car past this point would continue to the north end of downtown using Broadway and East Pike Street. *PNRA photo WWASMR-11-005 (Harold Hill, photographer).*

Route 12/Jefferson Park car #513 derailed at Twelfth Avenue South and South Massachusetts Street, 1939. Route 12, like Route 9, was a through-routed line with two outer terminals, Madison Park on the north and Jefferson Park on the south. In a scene captured by a *Seattle Post-Intelligencer* photographer, Jefferson Park car #513 was derailed and came within inches of striking a utility pole. No one was hurt. *PNRA photo WWASMR-12-015 (Museum of History and Industry collection).*

Route 12/Jefferson Park car #520 southbound on Twelfth Avenue South bridge, 1940. Jefferson Park passengers got a good view of downtown and First Hill as they crossed the Twelfth Avenue South bridge. *PNRA photo WWASMR-12-012 (Harold Hill, photographer).*

Route 12/East Madison car #508 on East Madison Street eastbound at Twenty-Fifth Avenue looking southwest, circa 1920. The Seattle Electric Company pushed the limits of electric streetcar braking and hill-climbing ability with the East Madison route. Originally built as a cable car line between downtown and Lake Washington in 1890, the company converted the eastern half of the line to electric car operation in 1910. Here, car #508 is heading downhill on a 14 percent grade with a full load of passengers. This group of cars was equipped with magnetic track brakes in addition to the regular wheel brakes, giving them extra stopping power. Sanders provided additional adhesion on the uphill grade. *PNRA photo WWASMR-12-046 (Museum of History and Industry collection).*

Route 13/Summit car #148 northbound on Summit Avenue at Howell Street, 1918. Small, single-truck "Birney" streetcars were introduced in Seattle during 1916, and the Summit line was fully equipped with them by 1918. Named for Charles O. Birney, a Stone & Webster engineer, the cars were designed to be operated by one person, a somewhat radical cost-saving idea at the time. Here, a Birney car pauses at Summit and Howell in the Capitol Hill neighborhood. *PNRA photo WWASMR-13-017.*

Southbound Route 13/Summit car #346 at Second Avenue and James Street with North Coast Lines bus, 1938. By 1931 all double-truck cars had been modified for one-person operation, so the small Birney cars lost their main economic advantage over the larger streetcars. When this photo was taken, the Summit line was using double-truck cars that were older than the single-truck Birneys they replaced. In this view, car #346 is nearing its downtown terminal while a North Coast Lines bus pulls alongside. *PNRA photo WWASMR-13-015.*

Route 14/Mount Baker car #581 at Hunter Boulevard South and South Hanford Street turnaround wye, with another car waiting, 1940. It is hard to imagine a more picturesque streetcar terminal than the one at Mount Baker, which used the landscaped median of Hunter Boulevard South as the south leg of the turnaround wye. An unidentified streetcar is waiting for car #581 to clear the east leg of the wye. The neighborhood, then as now, was filled with fine homes and well-kept lawns. *PNRA photo WWASMR-14-022 (Harold Hill, photographer).*

Route 14/Mount Baker car #286 eastbound at Thirty-First Avenue South and South Jackson Street, 1940. As Route 14 descended this hill, passengers were treated to a vista of Lake Washington before turning onto Thirty-First Avenue South. Rails were set in brick around this curve, encouraging motorists to slow down. *PNRA photo WWASMR-14-031 (Harold Hill, photographer).*

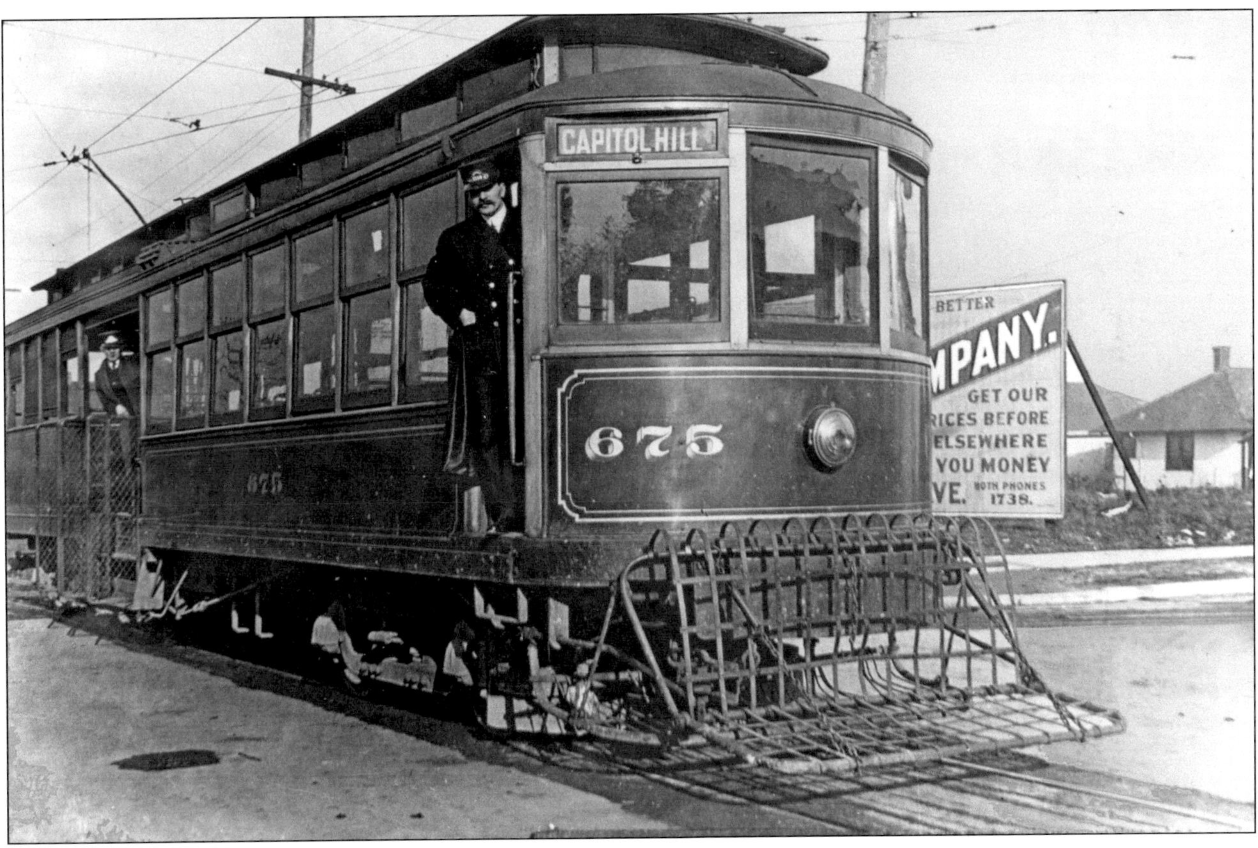

Route 14/Capitol Hill car #675 with crew at Volunteer Park turnaround wye, Fifteenth Avenue East and East Galer Street, 1910. The north end of Route 14 served Capitol Hill and ended at the main entrance to Volunteer Park. This early photo shows car #675 in its original configuration with an open-air section at the rear and a center entrance. By 1920 the open section had been enclosed and the passenger entrance was moved to the front. *PNRA photo WWASMR-14-038.*

Two Route 15/Broadway cars passing near Broadway and East Republican Street, 1931. Broadway was being widened when this picture was taken. Streetcars were operating on a single track in both directions through the construction area, using a siding to pass. The car numbers cannot be deciphered, but the smaller one on the right is a Birney car in the 100 series and the larger car is likely in the 500 series built by the St. Louis Car Company. The Birney is working a shorter version of the Broadway line that turned around at East Edgar Street rather than continuing all the way to the University District. *PNRA photo WWASMR-15-002.*

Route 15/Broadway car #399 at Harvard Avenue at Franklin Avenue East, 1940. The operator is standing by his streetcar, a 1907 American Car and Foundry product originally built for the Seattle–Everett interurban line. Looking at this intersection today, the view is dominated by the massive Interstate 5 Ship Canal Bridge. *PNRA photo WWASMR-15-006 (Harold Hill, photographer).*

Route 15/Broadway car #513 southbound on University Bridge, 1940. Just down the hill from the previous picture, the Broadway line crossed the University Bridge, sharing track with Eastlake Avenue Routes 16 and 17. The Red Cross has a patriotic display of American flags hanging from the trolley span wires. *PNRA photo WWASMR-15-011.*

Route 16/Ravenna car #281 eastbound on Ravenna Park private right-of-way near Twentieth Avenue NE, 1940. This was one of the most bucolic segments of Seattle's streetcar system, with tracks running on private right-of-way through Ravenna Park. Riders had a close view of the deep, heavily forested ravine, which was left in its natural state with old-growth timber and heavy underbrush. Here, car #281 is approaching the east end of the park and will soon reenter street right-of-way on NE Fifty-Fifth Street. *PNRA photo WWASMR-16-036 (Harold Hill, photographer).*

Route 16/Ravenna car #657 is leaving the west end of Ravenna Park where it will join Route 17 street trackage at Fifteenth Avenue NE and Cowen Place. *PNRA photo WWASMR-16-023 (Harold Hill, photographer).*

Route 16/Ravenna car #273 northbound on Eastlake Avenue at Fairview Avenue, 1940. Routes 16 and 17 shared the same path between downtown and the entrance to Ravenna Park, and these routes carried the highest volumes of streetcar passengers in the system. Here, car #273 passes Seattle City Light's Lake Union steam plant, built in 1911 to supplement the power produced by the utility's hydroelectric dams. *PNRA photo WWASMR-16-020 (Lawton Gowey, photographer).*

Route 17 car #270 is southbound on Fifteenth Avenue NE near Seventy-Fifth Street, in 1940. *PNRA photo WWASMR-17-005 (Harold Hill, photographer).*

Route 17 car #268 southbound at Fifteenth Avenue NE and Cowen Place, 1940. Routes 16 and 17 came together at this junction, located at the south end of the Cowen Park bridge. The track on the right led to Ravenna Park. *PNRA photo WWASMR-17-008 (Lawton Gowey, photographer).*

Route 18/Wallingford car #702 westbound on North Forty-Fifth Street at Meridian Avenue North, 1940. Route 18 connected three north end neighborhood business districts—the University District, Wallingford, and Fremont—before heading downtown. Here, a Route 18 car pauses to pick up a passenger in front of an A&P grocery store in the heart of Wallingford. *PNRA photo WWASMR-18-003.*

Route 19/Eighth Avenue NW car #710 inbound (southbound) at North Thirty-Fourth Street and Fremont Avenue North, 1938. Six streetcar routes funneled through the Fremont business district, making it the busiest junction in the system outside of downtown. In 1935, a streetcar passed through Fremont every minute or less during peak hours. The junction was a full "grand union," meaning that a right, a left, or a straight-through movement was possible from each leg of the intersection. Here, an Eighth Avenue NW car boards passengers heading downtown, and an outbound (northbound) Phinney car is visible up the hill in the distance. *PNRA photo WWASMR-19-015.*

Route 20/Green Lake car #752 at terminal, NE Seventy-First Street and Green Lake Way, 1937. The Green Lake line made a one-way counterclockwise loop around the lake, and streetcars paused here for a brief layover. The operator is speaking to the dispatcher on the Seattle Municipal Railway telephone while two passengers wait to board the car. The building on the right served as a waiting shelter and public restroom and remained in place until 2009. *PNRA photo WWASMR-20-037.*

Route 20/Green Lake car #756 southbound on Woodland Park trestle, 1937. To maintain easy gradients, builders of the Green Lake line constructed two trestles in Woodland Park. The southern trestle crossed rolling terrain in the center of the park and was frequently photographed with a "Seeing Seattle" streetcar full of happy passengers. The northern trestle, shown here, eased the gradient as streetcars climbed the hill from Linden Avenue into the park. The widening of Aurora Avenue and construction of a new North Sixty-Third Street underpass led to the demise of the Green Lake line in May 1937. *PNRA photo WWASMR-20-039.*

Route 21 Phinney car #527 at North Eighty-Fifth Street and Greenwood Avenue terminal wye, 1940. The operator of car #527 is pictured with another employee who helped get the streetcars safely turned around on the wye, halting motor vehicle traffic if necessary. The Grand Theatre in the background is still in use today as the Taproot Theatre, a venue for stage plays. *PNRA photo WWASMR-21-003.*

Route 21 Phinney car #534 southbound at Dexter Avenue and Westlake Avenue, 1940. A well-filled Phinney car has just crossed the Fremont Bridge on its way downtown, and will soon veer off the street onto private right-of-way following the Lake Union shoreline. The streetcar boarding area in the middle of the street is protected by a kiosk topped with a flashing light. The passenger shelter on the left survives to this day and now serves bus riders. *PNRA photo WWASMR-21-018 (Harold Hill, photographer).*

Route 22/Meridian car #757 southbound on private right-of-way underneath the Aurora Bridge, circa 1940. This view, taken about 1,000 feet east of the previous photo, shows a Meridian car operating on the Lake Union private right-of-way. *PNRA photo WWASMR-22-021.*

Route 23 car #201 southbound on Twenty-Third Avenue between Marion and Spring Streets, 1920. After 1931, Route 23 became the only streetcar route that did not serve downtown Seattle. Just 1.5 miles long, this rarely photographed route connected central Seattle neighborhoods along Twenty-Third Avenue. Its relatively light ridership made it a good candidate for the small one-man Birney cars like the #201 pictured. *PNRA photo WWASMR-23-001.*

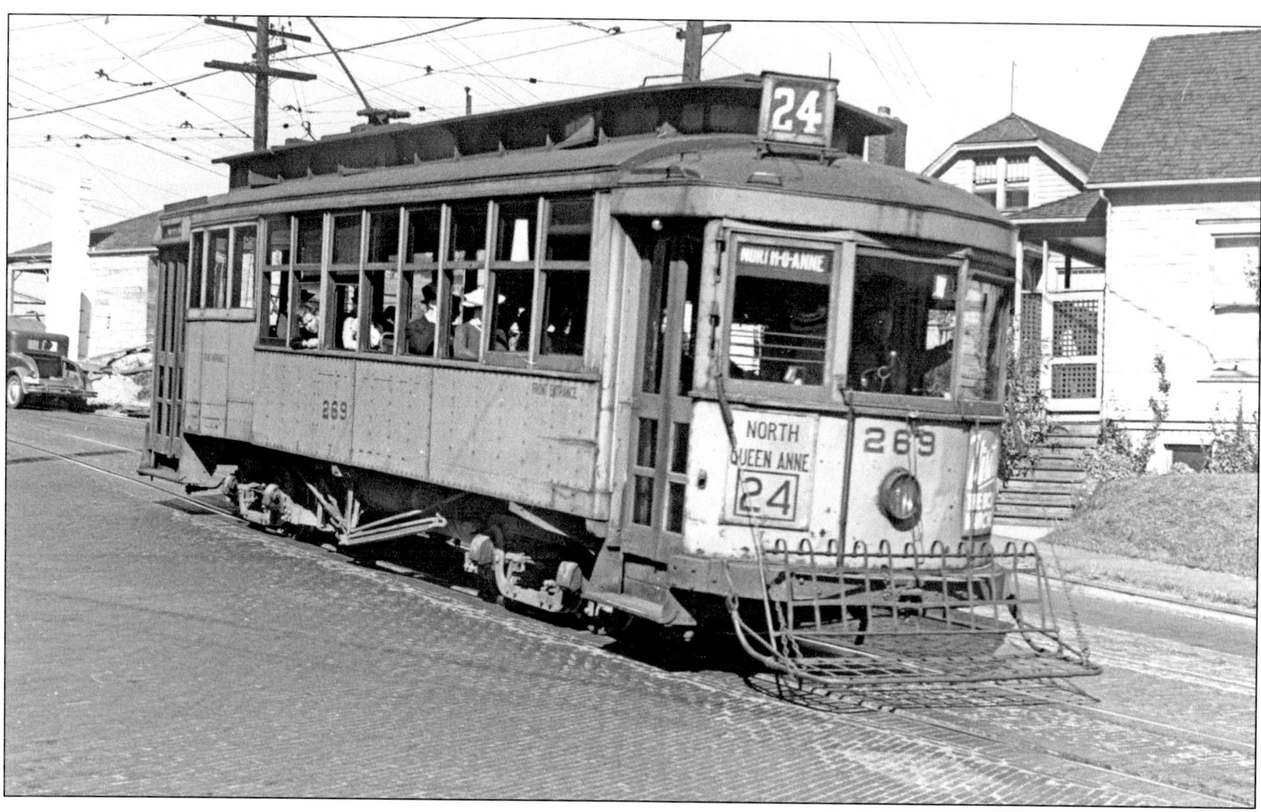

Route 24/North Queen Anne car #269 southbound on Taylor Avenue North at Galer Street, circa 1940. The 24/North Queen Anne and 25/East Queen Anne routes shared a common path between downtown and Queen Anne Avenue at Boston Street. This segment of Taylor Avenue was served by both routes, meaning a streetcar came by every seven to eight minutes for most of the day. *PNRA photo WWASMR-24-004.*

Route 24/North Queen Anne car #663 on Seventh Avenue West and West Raye Street, 1940. North Queen Anne cars turned around using a wye at Seventh Avenue West and Pleasant Place, then backed into a layover track across the street from the Mount Pleasant Cemetery. The entrance to the cemetery is shown on the left of this photo. *PNRA photo WWAST-24-019 (Harold Hill, photographer).*

Route 25/East Queen Anne car #277 southbound approaching terminal at Second Avenue North at Galer Street, 1940. Originally a shuttle route connecting with the counterbalance line at Queen Anne Avenue and Galer Street, Route 25 began through service to downtown in 1910 using a roundabout path via Queen Anne Avenue, Boston Street, and Taylor Avenue. A major source of riders was Queen Anne High School, a few steps east of the terminal on Galer Street. The houses to the right of the streetcar were demolished in the 1950s to make way for the school's athletic field, and the site later became the home of John Hay Elementary School after the high school closed in 1981. *PNRA photo WWASMR-25-003 (Harold Hill, photographer).*

Route 26/West Queen Anne car #314 southbound on Queen Anne Avenue at Highland Drive, 1940. To ascend or descend the steep 18 percent grade on Queen Anne Avenue, Route 26 streetcars were attached to a cable pulled by a gravity-powered "counterbalance" car running beneath the street. (Note the slot between the rails.) Cars #311 through #320 were equipped with hooks securely mounted to the front trucks, and a full-time helper was employed on the line to assist in attaching or detaching the cable from the hooks. *PNRA photo WWASMR-26-001 (Harold Hill, photographer).*

Route 26/West Queen Anne car #313 on Queen Anne Avenue northbound near Roy Street, 1940. The counterbalance operated for forty years, and it had a remarkably good safety record. But the infrastructure was costly to maintain and the operation was very labor-intensive. While counterbalance-assisted streetcar lines existed in a few other cities, Seattle's was the last one operating by 1940. In this view we see car #313 climbing the steep Queen Anne grade while a brand-new 1940 Chrysler is coming down the hill. *PNRA photo WWASMR-26-025 (Harold Hill, photographer).*

View of underground tunnel with counterbalance car, 1940. This is a rare view of the tunnel underneath Queen Anne Avenue showing the counterbalance car and its tow bar. Lighting was by kerosene lamp. *PNRA photo WWASMR-26-023.*

Route 27/Fifteenth Avenue NW car #730 inbound (southbound) on Dexter Avenue at John Street during Ballard Bridge closure reroute, 1939. The closure of the Ballard Bridge for construction in mid-1939 required rerouting Route 27 and 28 streetcars via the Fremont Bridge and Dexter Avenue. This photo shows a Route 27 car on Dexter, which at that time was a lightly traveled street with one-story buildings. Today this section of Dexter is marked by heavy traffic and high-rises. *PNRA photo WWASMR-27-026 (Harold Hill, photographer).*

Route 28 car #717 southbound on Loyal Way at Thirtieth Avenue NW, 1940. Running on track constructed in 1906 by Harry Treat's Loyal Railway Company, car #717 has just left the end of the line and is on its way to Ballard and downtown Seattle. Note that at this late date Loyal Way was still unpaved. The destination board shows the Fifteenth Avenue NW route in error. *PNRA photo WWASMR-28-034 (Harold Hill, photographer).*

Route 29/Fort Lawton car #807 southbound at the Gilman Avenue passing track, 1930. The lightly patronized Fort Lawton line was mostly single-track with streetcars running at infrequent intervals. In this wintertime view, car #807 is at the passing track located at Gilman Avenue and West Ruffner Street. *PNRA photo WWAST-29-001.*

Route 30/Sunset Hill car #586 southbound on Fremont Bridge during deck repair work, 1930. With its extremely heavy streetcar traffic, rails on the Fremont Bridge required constant inspection and maintenance. Here, a Sunset Hill car inches across the bridge while rail work is underway. *PNRA photo WWAST-30-006.*

Route 30 car #573 at Sunset Hill terminal, NW Sixty-Fourth Street at Thirty-Sixth Avenue NW, 1939. Originally called the Ballard Beach line, Route 30 ended at this turnaround wye with a sweeping view of Puget Sound and the Olympic Mountains. A few blocks down the hill was the dock for the Ballard–Indianola car ferry, a shortcut to the Kitsap Peninsula. *PNRA photo WWASMR-30-009 (James A. Turner, photographer).*

APPENDIX A
Seattle Municipal Street Railway Fleet Lists

Cable Car Fleet, 1937

Fleet Number	Builder	Year Built	Track Gauge	Type	Length	Notes
1–8	Hammond	1900	36"	Double-truck	28'1"	Enclosed and rebuilt 1913–14, assigned to Yesler line.
9–12	Hammond	1901	36"	Double-truck	28'1"	Enclosed and rebuilt 1914, assigned to Yesler line.
20–23	Seattle Electric	Circa 1907	36"	Double-truck	28'1"	Built at Georgetown shops. Enclosed and rebuilt 1914, assigned to Yesler line.
40 and 42–45	Stockton	1889	42"	Double-truck	31'2"	Enclosed and rebuilt 1910–15, assigned to Madison line.
46–49	Hammond	1896	42"	Double-truck	31'	Originally open-bench cars. Enclosed and rebuilt 1910–15, assigned to Madison line.
50	St. Louis	1889	42"	Double-truck	27'7"	Purchased from Omnibus Railroad & Cable Co. of San Francisco by Front Street Cable Railway. Enclosed and rebuilt 1914, assigned to James line.
51	St. Louis	1889	36"	Double-truck	27'7"	Purchased from Omnibus Railroad & Cable Co. of San Francisco by Front Street Cable Railway. Enclosed and rebuilt 1914, assigned to Yesler line.
60–61	Seattle Electric	1906	42"	Double-truck	28'	Originally single-end. Enclosed and rebuilt 1915, assigned to Madison line.
69, 71	Hammond	1901	42"	Double-truck	28'1"	Enclosed and rebuilt 1915, assigned to James line.
70	Hammond	1901	36"	Double-truck	28'1"	Enclosed and rebuilt 1915, assigned to Yesler line.
72–73	Seattle Electric	Circa 1907	42"	Double-truck	28'1"	Enclosed and rebuilt 1914, assigned to James line.
442	Stockton	1888	36"	Single-truck	15'5"	Still extant. Original Yesler open car from 13–15 series, assigned to maintenance-of-way duty after 1910. Currently in Museum of History & Industry collection.
443	Stockton	1888	36"	Single-truck	15'5"	Still extant. Original Yesler open car from 13–15 series, assigned to maintenance-of-way duty after 1910. Donated to Smithsonian Institution 1937.

Electric Streetcar Fleet, 1937

Car Types: ST = single-truck; DT = double-truck; SE = single-end; DE = double-end

Fleet Number	Builder	Year Built	Car Type	Length	Notes
110	Jackson & Sharp	1900	ST, DE	31'10"	Last of series, scrapped 1938.
143–167	American	1918	ST, SE	27'9"	Birney cars, scrapped 1938–1940.
168–182	American	1918	ST, DE	27'9"	Birney cars, scrapped 1938–1940.
183–184	American	1917	ST, DE	27'9"	Birney cars acquired from Spokane 1920, scrapped 1938–1940.
200–205	St. Louis	1919	ST, DE	27'9"	Birney cars, scrapped 1938–1940.
206–211	American	1919	ST, DE	27'9"	Birney cars scrapped 1938–1940 except car #210 body, now at Metro Employees Historic Vehicle Association.
260–285	St. Louis	1909	DT, DE	40'4"	Originally trailers, rebuilt as motor cars 1911. Scrapped 1940–1941.
286–299	St. Louis	1907	DT, DE	43'5"	Originally trailers, rebuilt as motor cars 1909. Last of series scrapped 1940–1941.
300–307	J. G. Brill	1900	DT, DE	40'	Last of series scrapped 1940.
311–320	Stephenson	1902	DT, DE	45'	Equipped for counterbalance service. Scrapped 1940–1941.
321–328	St. Louis	1902	DT, DE	45'1"	323, 324, & 326 sold to Puget Sound Electric Railway. Others scrapped 1940–1941.
323, 326	St. Louis	1906	DT, DE	46'8"	Originally from Bellingham. Second fleet with these numbers. Scrapped 1940.
332–347	St. Louis	1898–1899	DT, DE	44'6"	Acquired 1902 from Third Avenue Railway, New York City. All scrapped by 1940–1941.
348–349	Stephenson	1903	DT, DE	41'6"	Scrapped 1940–1941.
350–359	J. G. Brill	1900	DT, DE	42'2"	Originally open-bench cars. Enclosed and rebuilt 1901–1917. Scrapped 1940–1941.
362–365	Stephenson	1903	DT, DE	46'	Scrapped 1940–1941.
366–375	St. Louis	1898-1899	DT, DE	44'6"	Identical to 332–347. Acquired 1902 from Third Avenue Railway, New York City. Scrapped 1940–1941.
376–380	Jones	1904	DT, DE	44'8"	Scrapped 1940.
381–395	American	1905	DT, DE	43'10"	381–386 equipped for counterbalance service. Scrapped 1940–1941.
500–524	St. Louis	1906	DT, DE	43'9"	503–524 equipped with magnetic track brakes for use on East Madison line. Scrapped 1940–1941.
525–587	St. Louis	1907	DT, SE	44'6"	Originally with open section at rear, later enclosed. All scrapped by 1941.
602–651	St. Louis	1909	DT, SE	47'	Similar to 525–587 series. Scrapped 1939–1940.
630	PSTL&P	1917	DT, SE	49'8"	2nd car with this number, pilot for 723–727 series. Scrapped 1941.
652–661	St. Louis	1909	DT, DE	41'6"	Originally trailers, rebuilt as motor cars 1910; lengthened 1922–1923. Scrapped 1940–1941.
663–692	St. Louis	1909	DT, SE	47'	Originally with open section at rear, later enclosed. All scrapped by 1941.
700	St. Louis	1912	DT, DE	45'	Pilot for 701 series. Scrapped 1940.
701–710	Cincinnati	1913	DT, SE	49'2"	Scrapped 1940–1941.
711–722	St. Louis	1914	DT, SE	49'2"	Bodies identical to 701 series. Scrapped 1940.
723–727	PSTL&P	1917	DT, SE	49'2"	Similar to 701 series except front end. Scrapped 1941
730–741	Cincinnati	1914	DT, DE	45'	Originally purchased by Municipal Railway as 100–111. Scrapped 1940.
750–759	American	1918	DT, DE	46'	Originally trailers, rebuilt as motor cars 1920–1923. Scrapped 1940–1941.
800–824	Twin Cities Rapid Transit	1898–1899	DT, SE	43'11"	Originally Seattle Municipal Street Railway 300–324; acquired from Minneapolis for service during World War I. Scrapped 1939–1940.

MOTOR BUS FLEET, 1939

Fleet Number	Chassis Builder	Body Builder	Year	Model	Seats	Engine Placement*
30–49	Ford	Union City	1937	70	25	Cab-over-engine
92–101	Ford	Union City	1937	70	25	Cab-over-engine
107	Kleiber	Seattle Municipal Street Railway (SMSR)	1925	?	25	Conventional front engine
108, 110	Garford	SMSR	1923	51D	29	Conventional front engine
111–115	Garford	SMSR	1924	51D	29	Conventional front engine
117–120	Studebaker	SMSR	1925	?	21	Conventional front engine
122–126	REO	Fitzjohn	1926	W	21	Conventional front engine
127–131	Garford	SMSR	1926	KB	21	Conventional front engine
132–133	Garford	SMSR	1926	51D	29	Conventional front engine
134–135	White	SMSR	1926	50A	29	Conventional front engine
136–137	Studebaker	Studebaker	1927	?	21	Conventional front engine
138–144	Studebaker	Studebaker	1928	?	21	Conventional front engine
145–149	Mack	Mack	1928	AB	29	Conventional front engine
150	Studebaker	SMSR	1928	?	21	Conventional front engine
151	White	SMSR	?	50A	23	Conventional front engine
153–157	Mack	Mack	1930	BC	33	Conventional front engine
158–162	Mack	Mack	1931	BC	33	Conventional front engine
163	Fageol	Fageol	1931	?	38	Conventional front engine
164–165	Fageol	Fageol	1931	?	31	Conventional front engine
166–167	Kenworth	Kenworth	1931	BU	33	Conventional front engine
262	Twin Coach	Twin Coach	1935	30R	31	Rear engine
1131	Pacific Steel Coach	Pacific Steel Coach	1939	?	25	Rear engine
1401–1428	Twin Coach	Twin Coach	1937	30R	31	Rear engine
1701–1710	Kenworth	Tricoach	1938	H-30	38	Cab-over-engine
1801–1808	Twin Coach	Twin Coach	1937	40RC	40	Rear engine

*Note: "Conventional front engine" means the engine was mounted ahead of the body, similar to current highway trucks. "Cab-over-engine" means the engine was mounted inside of the body, adjacent to the driver's compartment. "Rear engine" means the engine was adjacent to rear axle.

APPENDIX B

Seattle Municipal Street Railway Service Levels, April 1939

Cable Car Routes

Route	Areas Served	Midday service intervals in minutes	Peak service intervals in minutes
James St.	First Hill, Downtown, Pioneer Square	12	12
Madison St.	First Hill, Downtown, Central Waterfront	6	4
Yesler Way	Leschi, Central District, Yesler Terrace, Downtown	9	6

ELECTRIC STREETCAR ROUTES

Route	Areas Served	Midday service intervals in minutes	Peak service intervals in minutes
1 Alki	Alki, Harbor Island, SODO, Downtown	20	15
2 Fauntleroy	Fauntleroy, West Seattle Junction, Harbor Island, SODO, Downtown	12	5
3 West Seattle	Admiral, West Seattle Junction, Harbor Island, SODO, Downtown	12	5
6 Nickerson–South Seattle	North Queen Anne, Dexter, Downtown, Georgetown	20	15
7 Kinnear	West Queen Anne, Lower Queen Anne, Downtown	12	9
8 Madrona	Madrona, Central District, First Hill, Downtown	12	10
9 19th Ave.–26th Ave. S	East Capitol Hill, First Hill, Downtown, Judkins Park	12	12
10 Montlake	University District, Montlake, Central District, First Hill, Downtown	12	10
11 East Cherry	Madrona, Central District, First Hill, Downtown	12	10
12 East Madison–Jefferson Park	Madison Park, Central District, First Hill, Downtown, Beacon Hill, Jefferson Park	10	8
13 Summit	West Capitol Hill, Downtown	12	10
14 Capitol Hill–Mt. Baker	Volunteer Park, Broadway, Downtown	15	8
15 Broadway	University District, North Capitol Hill, Broadway, Downtown	9	7
16 Ravenna	Bryant, Ravenna Park, U District, Eastlake, Downtown	10	8
17 15th Ave. NE	Maple Leaf, University District, Eastlake, Downtown	10	8
18 Wallingford	University District, Wallingford, Fremont, Westlake, Downtown	15	10
19 8th Ave. NW	West Woodland, Fremont, Dexter, Downtown	20	12
21 Phinney	Greenwood, Phinney Ridge, Fremont, Westlake, Downtown	9	5
22 Meridian	Meridian, Wallingford, Fremont, Westlake, Downtown	15	10
23 23rd Ave.	23rd Ave. between East Madison & South Jackson	20	20
24 North Queen Anne	North Queen Anne, East Queen Anne, Lower Queen Anne, Downtown	15	12
25 East Queen Anne	East Queen Anne, Lower Queen Anne, Downtown	15	15
26 West Queen Anne	West Queen Anne, Lower Queen Anne, Downtown	12	7
27 15th Ave. NW	Crown Hill, Ballard, Interbay, Downtown	15	10
28 Ballard–28th Ave. NW	Loyal Heights, Ballard, Interbay, Downtown	12	10
30 Sunset Hill	Sunset Hill, Ballard, Fremont, Dexter, Downtown	20	15

Motor Bus Routes

Route	Areas served	Midday service interval in minutes	Rush hour service interval in minutes
Alki–Admiral	Circle from West Seattle Junction & return via Beach Dr., Alki, Admiral & 35th & Avalon	30	30
Beacon Ave.	South Beacon Hill to Beacon & Lander via 15th Ave. S	30	20
Carleton Park	Fort Lawton to 15th & Galer via Viewmont Way	30	20
28th Ave. West	North Magnolia to 15th & Galer via 28th Ave. W	30	20
Ballard–University	Ballard to University District via Greenwood & Green Lake	20	10
Empire Way (Martin Luther King Jr. Way)	Rainier Beach to Downtown via Empire Way & Rainier Ave.	30	12
Roosevelt–40th St.	Maple Leaf to Wallingford via Roosevelt Way & N. 40th St.	30	20
Genesee St.	Columbia City to 50th & Dawson via Genesee St.	20	20
24th Ave. SW (Delridge Way)	White Center to 23rd & Spokane via Highland Park & 24th Ave. SW	20	8
3rd Ave. NW	Greenwood to 34th & Fremont via 3rd Ave. NW	30	15
NE 65th St.	Wedgwood to University District via 65th St., 20th NE & 45th St.	15	15
35th Ave. SW	Roxbury St. to Avalon Way via 35th Ave. SW	15	9
Laurelhurst–University of Washington	Laurelhurst to University District via 45th St. & Montlake Blvd.	60	20
Roosevelt Express	Maple Leaf to downtown via Roosevelt, Eastlake & Fairview	10	10
Pleasant Valley–South Park	Pleasant Valley to downtown via north/east Magnolia, Interbay, 15th Ave. W & Elliott Ave.	15	10
Laurelhurst Express	Laurelhurst to downtown via 45th St., Eastlake & Fairview	60	30
Rainier Ave.	Rainier Beach to downtown via Rainier Ave. & Dearborn St.	10	4
Seward Park	Seward Park to downtown via Beacon Hill & 4th Ave. S	30	20
East Green Lake	Green Lake to Downtown via Stone Way & Aurora Ave.	10	7
West Green Lake	Green Lake to Downtown via N. 80th St., Linden Ave. & Aurora Ave.	12	8
Highland Park Way	White Center to Downtown via Highland Park, W. Marginal Way	30	15

APPENDIX C
Annual Seattle Municipal Street Railway and Seattle Transit System Ridership, 1919–1941

Year	Streetcar & Cable Car	Motor Bus	Trolley Coach	Total Passengers
1919	133,235,932	—	—	133,235,932
1920	122,866,577	248,296	—	123,114,873
1921	97,156,839	362,374	—	97,519,213
1922	96,111,098	295,677	—	96,406,775
1923	97,171,756	791,934	—	97,963,690
1924	93,230,797	1,036,177	—	94,266,974
1925	90,940,414	1,517,424	—	92,457,838
1926	87,776,247	2,666,767	—	90,443,014
1927	85,625,809	4,997,589	—	90,623,398
1928	85,320,990	5,672,962	—	90,993,952
1929	83,095,998	6,033,716	—	89,129,714
1930	79,057,982	6,552,470	—	85,610,452
1931	70,214,632	7,630,148	—	77,844,780
1932	58,153,010	5,769,327	—	63,922,337
1933	54,401,119	5,486,951	—	59,888,070
1934	59,480,961	6,684,410	—	66,165,371
1935	59,116,395	6,989,328	—	66,105,723
1936	59,726,740	9,159,318	—	68,886,058
1937	58,040,437	15,456,463	—	73,496,900
1938	53,849,512	17,357,168	—	71,206,680
1939	52,684,912	17,670,234	—	70,355,146
1940	29,972,507	35,493,754	13,408,753	78,875,014
1941	1,823,030	37,372,105	51,956,342	91,151,477

Notes:

- The Seattle Municipal Street Railway and the Seattle streetcar properties of Puget Sound Traction, Light and Power were consolidated effective April 1, 1919.
- The Seattle Transit System replaced the Seattle Municipal Street Railway effective August 1, 1939. Streetcar service ended on April 13, 1941.
- Total passengers for 1939–1941 are from Seattle Transit annual reports; however, the breakout of passengers by mode of transportation for these years is estimated.

Acknowledgments

This book would not have been possible without the efforts of three individuals to document the last years of the Seattle Municipal Street Railway. The photographs by Harold Hill, James A. Turner, and Lawton Gowey in this volume give life to a remarkable era of Seattle history when most of the city's transit service was provided by a large fleet of "antique cars." Their contribution is priceless.

Leslie Blanchard's *Street Railway Era in Seattle* provided part of the inspiration for this book. I met Mr. Blanchard when he was doing research on Seattle streetcars at the Seattle Central Library, where I worked as a teenager. His detailed 1968 history of Seattle streetcars is still the last word on the subject and it got me thinking about how the story could be combined with quality photos and maps to give the reader more of a feeling of "being there."

Richard C. Berner's three-volume *Seattle in the 20th Century* filled many of the gaps in Blanchard's narrative, clearly explaining the political forces at work as the Municipal Railway struggled through the 1920s and 1930s. Berner's research helped me to pull the streetcar story together in one place.

I owe many thanks to Gary Tarbox and Bob Kelly of the Pacific Northwest Railroad Archive (PNRA), the source of most of the book's photographs. They encouraged me to undertake this project and provided valuable advice and recommendations as it moved forward. I also want to thank PNRA volunteers Kurt Armbruster and Rich Wilkins, who reviewed the first draft of the manuscript and offered excellent suggestions. PNRA volunteer John Mantle spent many hours scanning streetcar photographs for the book.

Mike Voris, who supervised King County Metro's bus procurement program for almost forty years, was a source of great inspiration in putting together the streetcar story. His collection of maps, vehicle specifications, fleet lists, and photos helped produce a more historically accurate work.

Other individuals who assisted me include Clay Eals, coproducer of the "Now and Then" feature in the *Seattle Times*; Leroy Chadwick, retired librarian at King County Metro Transit; Nancy Salguer McKay, director of the Highline Heritage Museum; Phil Stairs of the Puget Sound Regional Archives in Bellevue; and Jean Fulton, who researched the 1922 state supreme court decision that so impacted the Municipal Railway.

Thanks are also due to Bob Wodnik and Jim Moore, two former Sound Transit colleagues. Bob reviewed the first draft and wrote the foreword for the book. Jim, a fellow transit planner, provided me with copies of the Beeler consultant reports from the 1930s that rekindled my interest in Seattle streetcar history.

Finally, I owe much gratitude to Sophia Nelson and Dave Cooley, the two cartographers who produced the maps shown in the book. Sophia and Dave created one-of-a-kind route maps that give geographic perspective to the story of Seattle streetcars.

Notes

Chapter 1

1. For an overview of Burke's influence on Seattle's development, see Robert C. Nesbit, *He Built Seattle: A Biography of Judge Thomas Burke* (Seattle: University of Washington Press, 1961).

2. Clarence Bagley, *History of Seattle from the Earliest Settlement to the Present Time, Vol. 1* (Seattle: S. J. Clarke, 1916), pages 430–31.

3. For an excellent description of early streetcar technology, see William D. Middleton, *The Time of the Trolley* (n.p.: Kalmbach Publications, 1967).

4. George W. Hilton, *The Cable Car in America: A New Treatise upon Cable or Rope Traction as Applied to the Working of Street and Other Railways* (Berkeley, CA: Howell-North, 1971), front flap.

5. For a more detailed history of the Rainier Valley line, see Leslie Blanchard, "Trolley Days in Seattle: The Story of the Seattle and Rainier Valley Railroad," *Railway History Quarterly* 2, no. 2 (April 1965).

6. Robert C. Nesbit, *"He Built Seattle": A Biography of Judge Thomas Burke* (Seattle: University of Washington Press, 1961), page 265.

7. For a history of Seattle's early electric utilities, see Robert Carlyle Wing, ed., *A Century of Service: The Puget Power Story* (n.p.: Puget Sound Power & Light Company, 1987).

8. For an excellent description of the man-made changes to Seattle's landscape during this period, see David Williams, *Too High and Too Steep: Reshaping Seattle's Topography* (Seattle: University of Washington Press, 2017).

Chapter 2

1. Robert C. Wing, *A Century of Service: The Puget Power Story* (Bellevue, WA: Puget Sound Power and Light Company, 1987), pages 43–44.

2. Sharon A. Boswell and Lorraine McConaghy, *Raise Hell and Sell Newspapers: Alden J. Blethen & the Seattle Times* (Pullman: Washington State University Press, 1996), page 150.

3. For a detailed history of the municipal ownership movement in Seattle, see Richard C. Berner, *Seattle 1900–1920: From Boomtown, Urban Turbulence, to Restoration* (Seattle: Charles Press, 1991).

4. For a more detailed history of Harry Treat's streetcar line, see Ralph E. White, "Loyal Railway Company," *National Railway Historical Society Bulletin* 36, no. 2 (1971).

5. For more background on Birney streetcar operation in Seattle, see the "More Service, Less Cost" issue of the *Electric Railway Journal* 50, no. 12 (Sept. 22, 1917), pages 492–96.

6. Wing, *A Century of Service*, page 59.

7. For background on the history of organized labor in the streetcar industry, see *A History of the Amalgamated Transit Union* (Washington, DC: Amalgamated Transit Union, 1992).

8. Leslie Blanchard, *The Street Railway Era in Seattle: A Chronicle of Six Decades* (Forty Fort, PA: H. E. Cox, 1968), page 105.

9. Berner, *Seattle 1900–1920*, page 320.

10. Wing, *A Century of Service*, page 60.

11. "Car Makes Mad Dash Down Hill," *Seattle Daily Times*, October 28, 1919, page 1, and "Inquiry Begins When Car Wreck Victim Dies," *Seattle Daily Times*, January 6, 1920, page 1.

Chapter 3

1. *Asia v. City of Seattle*, 119 Wash. 675 (1922), Washington Supreme Court, No. 17132, 119 Wash. 674.

2. For the complete story of the Spokane Street bridges, see Myra L. Phelps, *Public Works in Seattle: A Narrative History [of] the Engineering Department, 1875–1975* (Seattle: Seattle Engineering Department, 1978).

3. For additional background on William Grose and the East Madison neighborhood, see Calvin F. Schmid, assisted by Laura Hildreth Hoffland and Bradford H. Smith, *Social Trends in Seattle*, University of Washington Publications in the Social Sciences, vol. 14 (Seattle: University of Washington Press, 1944).

4. "Editorial: *Times* Urges Close Study of Rapid-Transit Report," *Seattle Daily Times*, January 6, 1929, page 1.

Chapter 4

1. Richard C. Berner, *Seattle 1921–1940: From Boom to Bust* (Seattle: Charles Press, 1992), pages 126–27.

2. Cover letter from John A. Beeler to Seattle mayor and city council, *Report to the City of Seattle on Its Municipal Street Railway System*, December 10, 1935.

3. Robert S. Wilson, *Trolley Trails Through the West, Vol. 3* (Yakima, WA: Wilson Brothers, 1978), page 57.

4. Correspondence files of Municipal Railway Superintendent Albert E. Pierce, 1926–1940, Washington State Archives, Puget Sound Regional Branch, Bellevue, WA.

5. Correspondence files of Municipal Railway Superintendent Albert E. Pierce, 1926–1940, Washington State Archives, Puget Sound Regional Branch, Bellevue, WA.

6. "2 Die, 60 Hurt in Crash!," *Seattle Daily Times*, January 8, 1937, page 1.

7. Correspondence between the Board of Public Works and prospective motor bus and trolley coach builders, 1936–1937 (Mike Voris collection).

8. For a detailed account of Arthur Langlie's role in the conversion from rail to rubber, see Berner, *Seattle 1921–1940*.

Chapter 5

1. "Ballard Bridge Closes for Year," *Seattle Daily Times*, May 29, 1939, page 2; "New Streetcar and Bus Lines to Open," *Seattle Post-Intelligencer*, May 26, 1939, page 34.
2. Cover letter from John A. Beeler to mayor and city council that introduced *Report to the City of Seattle on a Plan for Modernization of the Seattle Municipal Street Railway with R.F.C. Financing*, August 31, 1939.
3. Stanley I. Fischler, *Moving Millions: An Inside Look at Mass Transit* (New York: Harper & Row, 1979), pages 149–150.
4. Many details of the rails-to-rubber conversion can be found in the Seattle Transit System annual reports for 1939, 1940, and 1941.
5. "Seattle's Streetcars End Service Record of 57 Years," *Seattle Daily Times*, April 14, 1941, page 22.

Chapter 6

1. The Beeler Organization, *Report to The City of Seattle on Its Municipal Railway System*, December 10, 1935, page 42.

Sources
and Recommended Reading

Newspapers and Periodicals

"Albert E. Pierce, Street Railway Aide in 1930's, Dies," *Seattle Post-Intelligencer*, June 26, 1959, page 29.

"More Service, Less Cost" issue of *Electric Railway Journal* 50, no. 12 (September 22, 1918), pages 492–96.

Blanchard, Leslie, "Trolley Days in Seattle: The Story of the Seattle & Rainier Valley Railroad," *Railway History Quarterly* 2, no. 2 (April 1965), 49 pages.

Engeman, Richard H., "Electric Streetcars in Seattle: The Lawton Gowey Photograph Collection," *Pacific Northwest Quarterly* 77, no. 2 (April 1986), pages 59–67.

White, Ralph, "Loyal Railway Company," *Bulletin of the National Railway Historical Society* 36, no. 2 (1971), pages 3–12.

Books

Bagley, Clarence. *History of King County, Washington*. Chicago: S. J. Clarke, 1929.

Berner, Richard. *Seattle 1900–1920: From Boomtown, Urban Turbulence to Restoration*. Seattle: Charles Press, 1991.

———. *Seattle 1921–1940: From Boom to Bust*. Seattle: Charles Press, 1992.

Blanchard, Leslie. *The Street Railway Era in Seattle: A Chronicle of Six Decades*. Forty Fort, PA: H. E. Cox, 1968.

Boswell, Sharon, and Lorraine McConaghy. *Raise Hell and Sell Newspapers: Alden Blethen & the Seattle Times*. Pullman: Washington State University Press, 1996.

Eals, Clay, ed. *West Side Story*. Seattle: West Seattle Herald/White Center News, 1987.

Hilton, George W. *The Cable Car in America: A New Treatise upon Cable or Rope Traction as Applied to the Working of Street and Other Railways*. Berkeley, CA: Howell-North, 1971.

Nesbit, Robert. *"He Built Seattle": A Biography of Judge Thomas Burke*. Seattle: University of Washington Press, 1961.

Peterson, Lorin, and Noah Cleveland Davenport. *Living in Seattle*. Seattle: Seattle Public Schools (high school civics textbook), 1950.

Phelps, Myra L., Leslie Blanchard, James R. Robertson, Claude E, Buckner, and Roy W Morse. *Public Works in Seattle: A Narrative History [of] the Engineering Department, 1875–1975*. Seattle: Seattle Engineering Dept., 1978.

Schmid, Calvin F., assisted by Laura Hildreth Hoffand and Bradford H. Smith. *Social Trends in Seattle*. Seattle: University of Washington Press, 1944.

Wing, Robert. *A Century of Service: The Puget Power Story*. Bellevue, WA: Puget Sound Power and Light Company, 1987.

Collections and Company Files

Puget Sound Power & Light Company records, 1925–1932, Washington State Archives, Puget Sound Regional Branch, Bellevue, WA.

Seattle Municipal Street Railway: Annual reports, ridership and revenue charts, track maps, appraisals, correspondence files of Superintendent Albert E. Pierce, 1926–1940, and engineering drawings of trackwork, carbarns, passenger shelters, and trestles. Washington State Archives, Puget Sound Regional Branch, Bellevue, WA.

Seattle Street Railway Route History, 1890–1941: compiled by Leroy Chadwick, King County Metro Library.

Seattle Transit System: Annual reports for 1939–1941, Seattle Public Library, Seattle, WA.

Consultant Reports

Estimated Results Obtainable from Rehabilitation and Refinancing of the Seattle Municipal Street Railway System. Beeler Organization, September 1935.

Report to the City of Seattle on Its Municipal Street Railway System. Beeler Organization, December 1935.

Letter to Underwriters. Beeler Organization, October 1936.

Report to the City of Seattle on a Plan for Modernization of the Seattle Municipal Street Railway with R.F.C. Financing. Beeler Organization, August 1939.

Miscellaneous

Seattle Street Car Guide. Seattle: R. L. Polk, 1918.

The Terminal Plan: An Improved System of Urban Transportation, Prof. Austin V. Eastman, University of Washington Engineering Experiment Station, Bulletin No. 5, 1938.

Twichell v. City of Seattle, Case No. 15247. Washington State Supreme Court ruling, March 1919.

Asia v. City of Seattle, Case No. 17132. Washington State Supreme Court ruling, April 1922.

Recommended Further Reading

Dorpat, Paul. *Seattle Now & Then*, vol. 1 (1984), vol. 2 (1987), and vol. 3 (1989). Seattle: Tartu Publications.

Dorpat, Paul, and Sherrard, Jean: *Seattle Now & Then: The Historic Hundred*. Seattle: Documentary Media, 2018.

Fischler, Stanley. *Moving Millions: An Inside Look at Mass Transit*. New York: Harper & Row, 1979.

Kershner, Jim. *Transit: The Story of Public Transportation in the Puget Sound Region.* Seattle: Documentary Media, 2019.

Middleton, William D. *The Time of the Trolley.* Milwaukee: Kalmbach Publications, 1967.

Turbeville, Daniel. *The Electric Railway Era in Northwest Washington, 1890–1930.* Occasional Paper #12. Bellingham, WA: Center for Pacific Northwest Studies, Western Washington University, 1978.

Warren, James R., Mary-Thadia D'Hondt, Museum of History and Industry (Seattle), Historical Society of Seattle and King County. *King County and Its Queen City: Seattle.* Woodland Hills, CA: Windsor Publications, 1981.

Williams, David. *Too High and Too Steep: Reshaping Seattle's Topography.* Seattle: University of Washington Press, 2015.

Wilson, Robert. *Trolley Trails Through the West, Vol. 2.* Yakima, WA: Wilson Brothers, 1978.

Wing, Warren. *To Seattle by Trolley: The Story of the Seattle–Everett Interurban and the Trolley That Went to Sea.* Pacific Fast Mail, 1988.

———. *To Tacoma by Trolley: The Puget Sound Electric Railway.* Edmonds, WA: Pacific Fast Mail, 1995.

Index

M

N

O

P

Q

R

S

T

U

W

Y

About the Author

Seattle native Mike Bergman worked as a transit planner for King County Metro and Sound Transit for more than 35 years and retired in 2016. He is president of the National Railway Historical Society's Tacoma chapter and volunteers at the Pacific Northwest Railroad Archive in Burien, Washington, where he has organized the archive's large collection of historic streetcar photographs. Mike publishes articles in railroad journals and gives regular presentations on rail history to heritage organizations and community groups.